Shifting Winds

Life with an Addict
Finding a PATH Forward

Kym Rupeiks

ISBN (9781737588306)

Published by The Pinnacle Advisors Group LLC – Publishing Division

Editor's Note
The Twelve Steps of Alcoholics Anonymous are reprinted with permission of Alcoholics Anonymous World Services, Inc. (AAWS). Permission to reprint the Twelve Steps does not mean that Alcoholics Anonymous is affiliated with this program. AA is a program of recovery from alcoholism only—use of AA's Steps or an adapted version in connection with programs and activities which are patterned after AA, but which address other problems, or use in any other non-AA context, does not imply otherwise. (Reprint of the Twelve Steps was granted June 29, 2021.)

DEDICATION

For helping me make this book possible I would like to first thank Stephen Panebianco, MD not only for his medical knowledge and input on the many layers and levels of the addiction process, but for his genuine caring to challenge me to understand what I brought to the dance. I continue to learn that when we expand our awareness of the forces that reside within, we have more awareness of choice in how we experience future moments. And thank you to my dear friend and editor, Judy Eddy.

This book is dedicated to me and all the family members who have experienced living with an alcoholic or addict.

TABLE OF CONTENTS

FOREWORD

Shifting Winds is a deeply inspiring journey of courage and transparency that infuses realism, struggle, pain, and introspection while gifting hope, healing, and practical insight. When Kym asked me to write the foreword to *Shifting Winds*, without hesitation I enthusiastically agreed knowing that what she interweaves through these pages will significantly impact the lives of numerous family members and partners of alcoholics or those with other addictions, and those who themselves suffer with addictive behaviors.

Having over thirty years of privileged clinical work with various forms of human suffering, including alcoholism and other addictions, depression, anxiety, anger, and PTSD, it became apparent to me that human suffering can often fuel and drive an unhealthy addictive relationship with something outside of oneself. Often the less than conscious goal of transiently shifting one's undesirable internal state is operative on some level. Unfortunately, as a result, what emerges is an unhealthy alliance and dependence on that "external object" for a desired state that has been shifted away from pain.

In *Shifting Winds*, the courageous openness that Kym brings to her expression is truly inspiring. It is sometimes said that "nobody gets a free pass" regarding the necessity to integrate one's prior experiences, pain, and even traumas that have emerged along their journey in order to be free for the present moment. Without awareness, introspection, and integration of operative forces that often lurk behind the scenes, we are destined to attract experiences and relationships to re-create an unlearned principle through further pain or trauma until the principle is ultimately transcended. We become willing dance partners in the co-creation of dysfunction. So what breaks the chain, what halts the dance? As Kym exemplifies in *Shifting Winds*, openness, intention, and courage are required to step back and more clearly see how we are approaching our life through subconscious forces that contribute to our undesired reality. Through further introspection, awareness, support, and healing, we can eventually embrace the realization that even when we may have been wronged along the way, we are NOT a victim. Otherwise, we exude victim consciousness and can be self-destined to attract and replicate the pattern of personal suffering while even contributing to the suffering of others.

In *Shifting Winds*, Kym reflectively and creatively immerses the reader into her thirty-nine years of life experience with her partner, Val. This includes moments that go back to eighth grade when they met, to when they eventually lived together as seniors in high school, through subsequent life chapters of marriage, professional expression, geographical relocations, entrepreneurship, and beyond. All of this unfolds through a gradual crescendo of progressive alcoholism decades in the making that was in part seeded from prior generations in both participants.

It takes great courage to openly explore the lens we consistently bring to our moments in order to more clearly glean what can be refracted from that lens in positive ways moving forward. And yet, Kym does not stop there. She also reflects deeply on how her formative pre-Val experiences played a role in her journey on a less conscious level that contributed to her ultimate "choice" of Val as her partner, and how such experiences punched her dance card of participation with Val for almost forty years. Kym also shares how she responded and at times reacted to certain shared moments, how she went into protective mode, how her engagement with other loved ones became restricted in some respects, how she at times closed down emotionally, and how she engaged in moments of pushback out of her own pent-up anger and survival pathways. And yet, as she went through her own PATH, she reached pinnacle moments of transcendence and timeless connection that she willfully shares as well.

Along the journey of *Shifting Winds*, the reader is also graced with practical understandings about alcoholism and addiction from both psychological and medical perspectives. Similarly, it was Edgar Allan

Poe who said in an 1848 letter the year before his tragic death at the age of forty: *"It has not been in the pursuit of pleasure that I have periled life and reputation and reason. It has been the desperate attempt to escape from torturing memories, from a sense of insupportable loneliness and a dread of some strange impending doom"* (italics added). Such understandings are effortlessly interspersed throughout Kym's shared life journey with Val, and provide those whose life has been touched by addiction with valuable information and perspective that can lead to healing insights and informed decisions.

Who of us has the courage to unabashedly investigate the at times distorted lens we bring to our journey to seek greater clarity to be freer in the present moment, free from prior conditionings that impact our perceptions, thinking, emotions, and behavior, let alone share that with the world? *Shifting Winds* truly gifts impactful breadcrumbs of insight that connect the reader to his or her own personal PATH while providing sustenance so forward movement can take place with awareness, courage, intention, healing, and ultimately transformation. This is the opportunity along one's PATH of healing whether one chooses to stay in a certain relationship or move forward down other life trajectories. The choice is ours to make, provided we become aware of choice in the first place while understanding the power, ramifications, and opportunities of choice as we chart our life PATH forward.

Stephen Panebianco, MD
MindBodyImmunity.org

INTRODUCTION

I wrote this book to help readers understand the life cycle of living with an alcoholic and to understand the changes both the alcoholic and the family members experience. Through my personal story of being married to an alcoholic, I give the readers, if they live with an alcoholic (or someone challenged by another substance or addiction), the understanding that they can empower themselves to live with, or detach with love from, an alcoholic. Through my story, my goals are that readers understand the behaviors of the alcoholic and the family members and understand that knowing yourself and learning what you can change and what is out of your control is critical in living with an alcoholic.

Life with an alcoholic is an emotional roller coaster, one with feelings that span from love to anger to rage. The poem "The Guest House" by the thirteenth-century Persian poet Rumi describes the home I have shared with an alcoholic.

This being human is a guest house.
Every morning a new arrival.

A joy, a depression, a meanness,
some momentary awareness comes
as an unexpected visitor.

Welcome and entertain them all!
Even if they're a crowd of sorrows,
who violently sweep your house

empty of its furniture,
still, treat each guest honorably.
He may be clearing you out
for some new delight.

The dark thought, the shame, the malice,
meet them at the door laughing,
and invite them in.

Be grateful for whoever comes,
because each has been sent
as a guide from beyond.[1]

In your darkest moments, when your heart feels tender and broken wide open, a good poem can soothe your soul. As you navigate through your life with an alcoholic, you may find this poem resonates with your experiences, serves to remind you to accept the thoughts and emotions passing through you, and encourages you to meet them with courage, awareness, and respect. I created the acronym PATH (Partnership, Anger, Tolerance, Healing) to define my life changes that mirrored the stages of alcoholism. Life with an alcoholic can take you down a PATH of Partnership that can include joy and love, but, eventually, you turn a corner on your PATH to Anger, and you stumble, losing your objectivity as you argue, feel shame, and assume more responsibilities. After walking along in Anger, you turn yet another corner on the PATH, leading you to Tolerance—giving in, giving up, and unhappiness—tolerating so much until you are simply surviving the experience. You have lost part of your authentic self, who you are and what makes you happy, all for the sake of feeling the burden of someone else's addictive actions. You are heartbroken. But you can turn yet another corner on your PATH, and you can move toward the promise of Healing.

It is your choice to step back and look at your life. Yes, it is essential to understand alcoholism and the addiction process, but it is equally as important to understand the reactions and responses to the addictive process the nonalcoholic family member experiences. As the alcoholic moves through the stages of alcoholism, you, the nonalcoholic family member, move through phases on the PATH (figure 1), which,

1. Rumi, "The Guest House," 109

interestingly, often parallel the stages of alcoholism. Each phase brings new emotions, actions, and reactions as you walk farther down the PATH of Partnership, Anger, Tolerance, and Healing.

Once you realize and acknowledge you are in the Tolerance phase, you must step back and ask, "Who am I? What makes me happy? How do I manage my life with an addict or change my life and move away from the addict?" Heartbreak is like a cleansing. These seemingly unwelcome guests in the guesthouse of your mind will scrub away at everything that is untrue or unhelpful, if you let them. And not to worry: being guests, they will eventually depart as well.

Seek understanding of addiction, your role in the process, and find a community of support that will allow you to be open (free of judgment) about your life, seeing it with clarity and objectivity. This is your life! You are not responsible for the addict. You are responsible for yourself and to be all that you can be, the best that you can be. Take back your freedom and authentic self. Just like my husband lost his authentic self, I too lost my authentic self: my ability to freely visit friends and family, to equally share in a partnership instead of always lifting up the partnership, to engage in social events without a time requirement always nipping at my heels, or to be open and discuss my situation with loved ones. Learn from my life with an alcoholic, and prepare yourself to invite the next houseguests to your home—freedom, joy, laughter, sharing, and love.

Chapter 1—Yesterday

DAY 1. It was September 13, 2017, in Tucson, Arizona. As most of the country was shifting from hues of green to vibrant yellows, oranges, and reds as a thin veil of cooler evenings blanketed the changing scenery, Tucson days, as in so many Southwestern cities, were awash in a brilliant blue sky and a heat that touches your face and then wraps itself around you. It is the familiar and comforting warmth of a soft winter blanket.

I was driving my husband's car, a silver 2013 Nissan 370Z. I slowly rolled to a stop at a red light. I waited to turn right, listening to the deep hum of the engine as the car sat idle. The traffic cleared and I turned east, pressing the gas pedal hard, causing the car to jump forward and accelerate; I was elated with the power and gave a little holler: "Go, girl!" I pressed down farther on the gas pedal, and the engine responded with a deep rumble and smooth acceleration, heading toward the Catalina Mountains. They were magnificent—jetting up from the desert floor to 9,000 feet, jagged peaks shimmering silvers and blue-grays with the bold sapphire sky framing their majestic poses. At 9:00 a.m., the sun, rising from behind the mountains, created an unusual color and depth in the mountains; it seemed as if I was peering through a magnifying glass, studying each crevasse and ridge. The mountains were truly breathtaking and always captivating.

I had been driving for ten minutes and was almost to the hospital when my phone rang. I answered the hands-free car speaker, and my husband, Val, asked in a sheepish voice, "Hello. Where are you?"

"I am driving to the hospital; I should be there in five minutes. How are you?"

Ignoring my question, he continued in a soft voice, "Will you bring me my glass hand pipe and a small bud? And my cigarettes?"

His request surprised me and sent a jolt down my spine. Was he serious? We had checked him into Oro Valley Hospital's acute care at 8:00 the night before, and he knew he could not smoke in a hospital. He continued telling me, "When you arrive, hide the pipe in your hand and pass it to me. Have some marijuana in the bowl. The nurses will let me go outside for ten minutes—as long as I promise to hurry right back and crawl into bed."

In years past, I would have explained why the nurses were not going to take the intravenous needle (IV) out of his hand and the heart monitor tabs off his chest and let him go outside for a quick pot break. I would have rationalized, argued, and perhaps yelled to reveal reality. Worn down, exhausted, and manipulated, I had tolerated his condition and accepted his reality—as well as my own.

Keenly aware something was terribly wrong with his thought process, I complied and assured him I would bring his pipe and cigarettes.

He continued to talk, and the more he talked, the faster he talked. Animated and enthused, like a young boy with a new toy. "Hello. It's all right," I heard him softly say.

"Kym," he said with a childlike exuberance, "He is peeking his head out and winking at me."

"Who is peeking his head out and winking?" I suspiciously asked.

"The puppy. He is peeking from behind the cabinet and winking. His eyes are big, round, and brown. He is cute. Oh, now he is hiding again. Hurry! Hurry! You need to see him."

"I will be there soon, and you can show me the puppy."

As I hung up the phone, I thought, *The hallucinations arrived quickly. I wonder if this is unusual.*

The hospital parking lot was nearly full except the far corner where a mesquite tree's low-hanging branches offered solace and shade. Parked, the car idled with a low hum as I sat feeling the cool air wash over my body. Val and I had had our twenty-fifth anniversary last month, and I thought, *How did our lives change so much in twenty-five years?* The high school sweetheart I married had been energetic, fun, and full of dreams for our future. He was no longer that man. He was miserable and felt he had nothing left in life to look forward to—no more dreams. And I was no longer the person he married.

The visions of checking Val into the hospital yesterday danced in my thoughts. He had awakened early yesterday morning and had gently touched my shoulder as I lay asleep. Eyes still closed, I listened as he explained he was feeling immense pressure around his midsection. I opened my eyes to see him lifting his white T-shirt to his pectorals, revealing his bloated abdomen. His midsection was swollen around to his backside. He stood in his underwear, unable to pull pants up over his abdomen. The swelling extended down to his groin and caused his penis to shrink and disappear under his low-hanging belly. He was scared.

A few days earlier, his general practitioner, Dr. K., had prescribed diuretics for his edema, which is swelling caused by excess fluid trapped in the body's tissues. It is often the result of medication or underlying disease—often congestive heart failure, kidney disease, or cirrhosis of the liver. I suspected it was cirrhosis of the liver and so did Val's doctor. For the past year, Dr. K. had been telling Val his liver was swollen and that he needed to stop treating the symptoms and treat the disease.

Val called Dr. K. that morning and asked why his diuretics were not working. Listening to a one-sided conversation, I heard Val explain his symptoms and inquire why he was not improving. Val was silent for a few minutes while listening to Dr. K. Saying goodbye, Val disconnected the call. He turned in his chair, and with a wave of his hand, he sternly said, "Dr. K. believes I should go to the emergency room. I am not going to the emergency room. They will tell me I have a heart condition, and they will want to operate on me."

Val knew this because two years ago he had gone to the emergency room for a deep vein thrombosis (DVT), and the triage medical staff had been concerned with his high blood pressure and irregular heartbeat. When he had realized the triage was giving his heart issues priority and they would keep him overnight for observation, he had become anxious and had promptly left the hospital against medical advice. He never admitted the reason for his fear of a hospital or the medical community. Oh sure, he found reasons to fear hospitals—his mother had had complications after a hip replacement, friends had had less than pleasant experiences in the hospital, and I had spent a week in the hospital after developing pneumonia—but those were all others' experiences that he told as elaborate, embellished stories in his attempt to deny himself the truth: the truth that the effects of chronic alcoholism would invade every hiding place in his body as his brain and body struggled to coexist during the onset of alcohol withdrawal.

I calmly reminded him, "You cannot wear pants or shorts, and you cannot sit down without discomfort." Not knowing for sure, I confidently told him that if we went to the emergency room, they would admit him and give him diuretics intravenously—after all, I had read about edema on WebMD. I assured him that the intravenous solution would work quickly and he would be back home the same day. He needed this critical guarantee that he would return home by 5:00 p.m. so he could relax and surrender himself to his siren, the beautiful liquid that lured him to the bottle every night, just as the mythical sirens lured unwary sailors with their enchanting singing to shipwreck on the rocky coast. She beckoned him from the depths of his pink plastic tumbler of Canadian Club and 7UP. She always delivered the promise of serenity, and not a single day in the past twenty-five years had been lost to abstaining from her summoning. The urgency was apparent, and it was imperative he be assured he would return home the same day.

He agreed to go to the hospital. I did not pack an overnight bag for him because to do so would have panicked Val into thinking he would miss 5:00 p.m.; thus he would nix the hospital trip. I drove him to the emergency room, and we checked in around 2:00 p.m. A few hours later, a miracle that he waited, a nurse arrived and escorted us from the waiting room to a private room behind the large metal doors guarding the emergency area.

A triage nurse entered the room, politely introducing herself and smiling at Val as she asked him to explain the reason for his visit. He pushed down his loose-fitting basketball shorts, exposing his swollen abdomen and groin area. She then took his vital statistics (vitals) of temperature, respiratory rate, pulse, blood pressure, and blood oxygen saturation; his blood pressure was 180 over 140. Immediately, the edema took a back seat to the high blood pressure, just as the DVT had during the hospital visit two years earlier. She hooked Val to heart monitors and performed an EKG. She read the EKG results and confirmed that Val had atrial fibrillation (AFib)—a fast, irregular heart rhythm. Abnormalities or damage to the heart's structure are the most common causes of AFib, but other possible causes include high blood pressure, heart attack, lung diseases, and even exposure to stimulants, such as tobacco and alcohol. I wondered which condition he had had longer, an addiction to alcohol or AFib. He had taken a stress test for his heart in 2004 and had passed; therefore, he had been an alcoholic before having AFib. The odds that the alcohol consumption had caused his AFib were significantly high.

Val became agitated that the emergency room staff was focused on his heart. It was 6:00 p.m., and the hospital staff had taken no steps to treat his edema. He was ready to leave the hospital—to follow the song of the siren luring him in for his first drink. It was all he could think about: eagerly taking the first large gulps of his drink with his left hand as he held a cigarette between two fingers of his right hand. The first gulp was the most satisfying—nearly euphoric. Watching his ritual each evening, I knew the pleasure the first swallow of alcohol gave him—his shoulders softened and dropped down, relaxing as the alcohol coursed through his body. Taking a deep breath, holding, then exhaling out, the tension in his face disappeared as each tiny muscle relaxed and let go of the day.

The emergency room doctor entered. He told Val his magnesium was extremely low, and with AFib, they needed to keep him overnight to administer magnesium and monitor his heart. Exasperated, Val angrily said, "I have white-coat syndrome, and my blood pressure always goes through the roof when I see doctors."

The doctor calmly replied, "This is not a matter of being nervous during a visit to the doctor. You have been here for a few hours, your blood pressure remains elevated, and you have AFib. And your magnesium is dangerously low—life-threatening."

Val snapped at the doctor, "I don't need to stay overnight; my heart is fine. You just want to make money off me. I am not staying. I will come back tomorrow for treatment."

My jaw dropped open as I listened to my husband behave like a jackass. I thought, *He needs a drink, and now!*

The doctor was surprised but remained remarkably calm. "We are here to help people, and your life is in danger. You can choose to leave the hospital against medical advice, but I strongly advise that you stay."

He thought for a moment and continued, "If you leave now and come back tomorrow, we have to close this case and start the process over again."

Before Val could say another word, which was not going to be sensible but most certainly snarky, I asked the doctor to give us a minute and to leave the room. He nodded and left.

I looked at Val and said, "You are being a jerk. Your heart and edema need medical attention, and you want to go home. What is wrong with you?" Before he could reply, I continued, "Besides, if you leave against medical advice and then start the process over tomorrow, our insurance is not going to pay for two visits to the ER. Your decision will cost us thousands!"

He looked at me with disgust and said, "All right, I will stay tonight. Tell the doctor."

I turned to leave the room and thought to myself how lucky I was to find something that mattered enough to Val to stay in the hospital. It certainly was not his health. It was money. He knew how much his drinking and poor health was costing us. And I knew he did not care about anything or anyone except his beloved alcohol; he certainly did not care about me—I was a tool to further his addiction. If we had financial troubles, his daily drinking would be at risk, or at least the ease and accessibility of drinking.

I walked down the hallway and found the triage nurse and doctor. "Val will stay the night," I said.

"Good," replied the doctor. "We will get him upstairs into acute care as soon as possible." The doctor looked at me for a moment as if to tell me something, but then he walked away. I went back to Val's room to wait with him. By 10:00 p.m., a nurse had moved him from the emergency room to the fourth floor's acute care.

A middle-aged, physically fit nurse wheeled in a mobile laptop and introduced himself as Gary. We both introduced ourselves, and Gary gave Val a comforting and reassuring smile. He asked Val about family medical history, personal medical history, and medications. Val replied to each question, though he left out his family history of alcoholism and his own abuse of alcohol. As I listened to Val and Gary, I thought about his family history with alcohol as well as my own family history. Val had one alcoholic parent and grandparent, and both my parents were alcoholics. How was it that I'd grown up with alcoholic parents and then married an alcoholic? I wish I knew the answer—and how important of a role alcoholism had played in my formative years and marriage.

Val asked, "How will you treat the edema?"

Gary replied, "We will start you on treatment for your edema, but we have to stabilize your heart too. We need to control the AFib and give you magnesium."

Val nodded. I could see the worry in his expression. His silence and eyes revealed his angst. Was he thinking about his next drink and having it at home by this time tomorrow? He avoided discussing his alcoholism. I too said nothing, electing to not divulge any information to Gary about Val's drinking—it was no longer my responsibility—nothing was going to change. What had once been a dynamic partnership had slowly unfolded into moments of anger followed by tolerance, acceptance, and survival. It would be a few years later that I would learn and appreciate that Val's actions were not my responsibility to amend, alter, or deny—but that day, I enabled him to stay on a pathway of progressive alcoholism. Along that path, I had endured a trap of trying to live for two instead of one, myself, and yet I had struggled with the situation alone, unable to share with others who could possibly offer understanding and support. We had gone down the pathway of alcoholism together, hand in hand.

I believed Val would be released the next day and that he would be home before withdrawals from going "cold turkey" commenced. Had I too fallen into the trap of denial? I did not tell Gary that, a few months before, Dr. M. at the Scottsdale Mayo Clinic had told Val he believed his symptoms were due to alcohol. No, I wasn't in denial about Val's alcoholism, but I was in denial about the extent of the damage his body had endured over the years. By the time I had noticed the physical symptoms, the inside of his body had undergone incredible hardship.

If we do not change our direction,
we are likely to end up where we are headed.
—Chinese Proverb

CHAPTER 2—MAYO CLINIC

Almost a year ago, we were driving to our favorite Mexican restaurant, a small place with views of the Catalinas and the best homemade margaritas in town. It was fall and the days were shorter. Night had fallen, and beyond the reach of the car's headlights was an inky-black darkness with no streetlights to guide the way. Orange construction cones lined both sides of the roadway—it was difficult to see our lane, and oncoming headlights cast shadows and confusion. We pulled up to an intersection as the light turned from red to green. Our lane was diverted to the right, and Val slowly moved into the intersection while searching for our lane obscured between yellow flashing cones. He slowly picked up speed to thirty-five miles an hour. While fiddling with the radio station, I noticed the car was drifting to the right. The car hit the soft desert sand. As though in slow motion, we were heading toward desert shrubs and saguaro cactus. I looked at Val—his head was slumped over to the right, and his eyes were closed. In a panic, I yelled, "Val, wake up. You fell asleep!"

I grabbed the steering wheel and turned the car toward the street while attempting to escape the soft sand before the car tires were in too deep. At the same time, Val opened his eyes. Dazed, he replied, "I am not asleep. I just nodded off for a second." He placed his hands back on the steering wheel and started to drive again as the car regained traction on the paved road.

"You need to pull over and let me drive!" I demanded.

"I am fine. I am awake," he sheepishly replied.

We were less than a mile from the restaurant, and he finished driving us there. We opened our doors and got out of the car. I walked over to him and blurted out, "There is something very wrong with you, Val. You could have killed both of us. I am never letting you drive me again."

Surprisingly, he did not argue. Looking down at the pavement, he slowly handed the car keys to me, as though he was handing me his will to live. I felt his sense of loss as he released the keys into my palm. Feeling his anguish, I hesitated to speak, but then shared my concern and said, "You have to see a specialist. You have balancing issues and leg pain, and just now you fell asleep while driving. Something is seriously wrong."

He shrugged.

The next day, I started researching neurologists—I knew he would do nothing to help himself, and I couldn't stop trying to help him. My stepping aside would become a lesson to be learned and seldom applied.

As the months passed, Val couldn't walk in a straight line, often using hallway walls or other obstacles to balance his gait. The pain he experienced in his legs became unbearable at times. His feet felt like he was walking on pins, and the sensation would shoot up from his feet to his knees. Sometimes moving each foot forward was like trudging through cement. Simple movements were exhausting. To alleviate the pain, he tried medical marijuana and all the oils and foods made with marijuana. That didn't help. He then went to Pima Pain Center and tried oxycodone. The symptoms continued.

Our first visit to Mayo Clinic was in early May, several months after the car incident. We drove to Scottsdale for an early 9:00 appointment with Dr. M., a specialist in neurology and psychiatry. I dropped Val off at the entrance and drove into the underground parking garage. Parking next to the elevator, I quickly found the main level. I pulled open the entrance door while I scanned the lobby for Val. Spotting him seated next to the escalators, I walked to him and motioned to him to stand up while telling him we were going to the third floor. He put his cane, a recent purchase, in front of his knees, made sure it was stable, and lifted himself to his feet. He steadied his balance and then began the arduous task of walking to the elevators, bypassing the escalators; he wasn't sure-footed enough to maneuver onto an escalator.

The elevator doors opened, and we walked into the waiting room. We stood in a short line to check in. I tried not to stare at the young woman in front of us as her entire body shook. She couldn't control her shaking. As she walked, it was all she could do to move one foot forward and then the next. I was amazed at her tenacity, and thought, *My husband has self-induced balance and pain symptoms, and all he does is complain or blame others for his woes. Where is his tenacity? His self-determination?*

The help desk was efficient, and we were checked in for his appointment in less than ten minutes. The room was full of visitors yet eerily quiet. People were busy filling out paperwork, stopping briefly to whisper to their companions. We sat in silence. Val was obviously nervous, and I knew there was no reason to agitate him with wondering what his doctor would be like or guessing about the outcome of his appointment. Within fifteen minutes, a young man opened a side door and called, "Val." We stood up and made our way to the door.

The young man greeted us and took us down a brightly lit hallway with blue-green carpeting and soft-gold-painted walls. He stopped us at a scale and weighed Val, measured his height, and then politely escorted us into an exam room. The room was stylishly decorated with warm colors and two oversized, comfortable chairs. Next to the chairs was a desk, a rolling stool, and a computer. We sat down in the chairs and waited for Dr. M.

The doctor entered the room a few minutes later. He was of medium height, with dark brown hair and a lean build, much like a long-distance runner. He smiled and extended his right hand to introduce himself.

He looked straight into Val's eyes and said, "Tell me about yourself and what brings you to Mayo Clinic today."

Making a deep sigh, Val looked at me and said, "Huh, where do I start?"

"From the beginning," replied Dr. M.

Val started to share his timeline of events. "Let's see," he said. "I guess it started in 2013 when my feet started to tingle. I hated wearing socks. After a year or more, it felt like I was standing on marbles cut in half." He sighed and continued, "The tingling started moving up my legs to my knees. Then the tingling turned to pain. In 2015, I had a DVT in my left calf, and I couldn't walk for more than five minutes." He took another deep breath, exhaled with a snort through his nose, and continued, "By the summer of 2016, the tingling in my feet turned to numbness. The pain in my legs increased. It hurt to stand or sit but not to lie down, and I started losing my balance. I walk with a wide gait and sometimes use the walls or counters to balance myself." He looked up at Dr. M., and with a pitiful look and a plea in his voice, he said, "I just want the pain to stop or even be half of what it is now."

Dr. M. typed notes into his computer as Val explained his symptoms. Dr. M. then asked a series of questions about general health, family history, accidents and trauma incidents, and drug and alcohol use. Val replied to the series of questions but hesitated to answer the last question: "How much alcohol do you drink?"

Dr. M. noticed Val's hesitation to answer the last question and asked again, "How much alcohol do you drink a day or a week?"

"I have a few drinks each night," Val replied.

"What is a few?" Dr. M. inquired.

Val hesitated, and I turned and looked directly in his eyes. "Val, we are here to get medical help. You need to tell him how much alcohol you drink each day," I firmly insisted.

Dr. M. rolled away from his computer desk and turned to face Val. He had an inquisitive expression, one luring Val to be honest and talk to him.

Val sighed and said, "I have two large drinks a night, sometimes three. Alcohol is the only thing that helps my pain."

"How much alcohol is in a drink?" Dr. M. asked.

Anxious for Val to face his problem, I intervened and pressed Val to be honest and answer the question.

"About nine ounces of whiskey in each drink," he quietly replied. "I average twenty ounces of alcohol a night."

Doctors are typically reserved and try to maintain the utmost professionalism, but Dr. M. couldn't conceal his surprise. His eyes widened, and he sarcastically said, "Twenty ounces a night? Are you drunk now?"

I snickered. Val did not.

Dr. M. rolled back over to his keyboard and typed more notes. As he typed, he said, "Alcohol can affect the liver."

"My liver is fine," Val snapped. "I have been to my primary care physician. He has not recommended any tests, and drinking hasn't caused any problems."

A lie, I thought. But I wasn't privy to their doctor-patient conversations; however, Val never shared any details about alcohol or the effects of alcohol with anyone, so I presumed he hadn't told his doctor either. No, his physical problems were never related to alcohol. He would tell me, "No one can prove that alcohol is the cause of my physical pain—and if it can't be proven, then why blame it on alcohol?" An excuse I had heard many times.

"It isn't a problem until it is a problem," Dr. M. said a tad sarcastically. He stopped typing and gazed at Val for a minute with bewilderment, as he likely understood Val's health symptoms were a result of his own actions—indulgence in alcohol. He typed a few more notes into the computer and then rolled his chair back and stopped in front of us.

"All right," he said. "I want to perform a series of examination tests to evaluate your neurological functions."

"Will we do these tests in your office?" Val asked.

"Yes," Dr. M. replied. "We will start the neurological evaluation with some simple tests to assess your neurological function and your ability to feel different sensations. I want you to close your eyes, hold up your right index finger, and then touch your nose with the finger."

Val complied. He held up his right index finger and then moved the finger to his nose. He missed and touched the crease between his nose and cheek.

The doctor instructed him to perform the same test, but touching his forehead, chin, and other body parts. Each time Val complied, and each time he failed to touch the correct area, spurring Dr. M. to enter the action and result into his computer.

Dr. M. then held up his own right index finger and told Val to follow his finger. The doctor moved his finger left, then right, then up, and then down. Each time, Val followed his finger.

"Good," Dr. M. said. "Now I am going to give you three words to remember, and at the end of our visit, I am going to ask you to repeat the three words."

Val nodded, showing interest in this test. It was an opportunity to prove to me and the doctor that his mind was functioning fine despite the fact that his body had been slowly deteriorating.

Dr. M. said, "The three words I want you to remember are pencil, watch, and chair. Will you repeat those three words to me?"

Val nodded. "Pencil, watch, and chair," he said confidently.

"Good," Dr. M. said. "Now I am going to perform some tests to evaluate your sensation and reflexes."

Dr. M. pulled a pen out of his pocket and slowly stroked the bottom of each foot in a curved line from the heel up toward the toes and over to the big toe. First the right foot and then the left. Val didn't wiggle or giggle as his feet were lightly touched with the pen. He didn't move his body in response to any sensation. Dr. M. rolled his stool over to the computer desk and typed more notes.

He then turned back to Val and said, "Now I want you to close your eyes. I am going to bend your toes one at a time. I am going to bend them up or down, and I want you to tell me which way I am bending them." Val nodded and closed his eyes. Dr. M. moved each toe, sometimes moving the toe up first and then down, or moving the toe down first and then up. Val was able to tell when the smaller toes were being bent up or down, but he did not respond to the doctor moving his big toes up or down; he was unaware the doctor had moved them. Again, Dr. M. typed more notes.

"Now let's test your coordination. I want you to sit on the edge of your chair and lift your right foot to your left knee and slide the foot down your left shin to your left foot," Dr. M. requested.

Val sat up straight and slid to the edge of his chair. He raised his right foot and could not place it to his left knee. His right leg was shaky, and the right foot landed just below his left knee and to the inside of his shinbone. He tried to slide the knee down the side of his leg, but his foot fell off and landed on the floor. He tried to do the same with his left foot to his right knee. Again, he missed his knee, and his foot slid off his shin and to the floor. He failed the test with both feet.

Dr. M. stood up from the stool, grabbed a straight-backed chair, and pushed it to face Val. He instructed Val to stand up and bend forward. "Use the back of the chair for balance if you need support. I don't want you to fall forward and hurt yourself," he said with a smile.

Val stood up and took two steps forward to the chair. He bent forward, and his upper body tilted off to the side. Val quickly grabbed the back of the chair to steady himself. He regained his balance and tried again. He slowly bent forward, lost his balance, and tilted to the side. Again, he grabbed the back of the chair to balance himself.

"Now I want to watch you walk down the hallway, turn around, and walk back to me," Dr. M. instructed.

Val reached for his cane that was leaning against the chair.

"No, I would like you to walk down the hall without the cane," Dr. M. said.

Val complied and slowly walked to the door. He grabbed the edge of the door for balance, then let go and walked down the hallway. Dr. M. watched him walk down and back. I was still sitting in my chair and couldn't see Val perform the test, but I knew he walked like a drunken sailor leaving the harbor bar—swaying from side to side as he fought with all his might to keep walking in a straight line.

Val came back into the room and sat in his chair. Dr. M. took his place on the stool and resumed typing. He then turned to Val and asked, "What are the three items I asked you to remember?"

Val gleefully said, "Pencil, watch, and chair."

"Correct!" Dr. M. said. He finished typing notes and then turned to address both of us.

"Your lack of balance is called ataxia, which is a loss of full control of voluntary body movements. Ataxia can affect various movements, creating difficulties with speech, eye movement, and swallowing. Persistent ataxia usually results from damage to the part of your brain that controls muscle coordination—the cerebellum."

I interrupted and asked, "What causes ataxia?"

Dr. M. replied, "Many conditions can cause ataxia, including alcohol abuse, certain medications, stroke, tumor, cerebral palsy, brain degeneration, head trauma, certain nutrient deficiencies, and multiple sclerosis. Inherited defective genes can also cause the condition."

"I've had head trauma," Val declared. He turned to look at me and continued, "Remember the time in the driveway when I was trying to compression-start my motorcycle and I fell over with the bike? I didn't have my helmet on and I hit my head."

I looked at him with a puzzled expression. "You think head trauma caused your ataxia?" I asked. I thought, *The doctor just told you the first cause of ataxia is alcohol abuse. You don't think all this shit is due to your alcoholism? Are you an idiot or just refusing to admit you are an alcoholic?*

Dr. M. ignored Val's recount of the motorcycle incident and

continued, "I am going to order some tests so we can rule out or identify the cause of your ataxia. I will order lab work so we can check your blood for vitamin deficiencies, toxic elements, and evidence of any abnormal immune responses. It would be a good idea to have an MRI of the brain as well as an electrodiagnostic test to measure the electrical activity of the muscles and nerves." He paused and then continued, "All those tests can be performed here at Mayo Clinic, and perhaps they can be scheduled today."

Val scrunched his nose and huffed. "Today? It will take all day."

"Yes, but it will be done in one location, by our specialists, and we can evaluate the results."

"I don't want to stay here all day," he snapped. He was becoming increasingly agitated and didn't seem to mind that he was behaving like a petulant child.

"Val, we are here, and it will be easy to coordinate and complete the tests in one place and in one block of time," I said.

"No, I am going home and will have the tests done in Tucson or come back another day," he persisted.

"I strongly recommend the lab work and the electrodiagnostic test be performed here," Dr. M. said. "I know the process and the doctors' knowledge and prefer that they be performed here."

Val shrugged. "All right. I will stay for those tests and have the MRI in Tucson," he said. "It will be cheaper to have the MRI in Tucson."

Dr. M. stood up and left the room to order the two tests. Val and I sat quietly and waited for him to return. I stared straight ahead, in my own world, thinking, *Cheaper? You don't want to stay for three tests because we wouldn't get home until after seven and you wouldn't be able to have your first drink at five. Tick tock, tick tock, you have to have your drink at five o'clock.*

The urgency for his first drink had started a little over twenty-five years before. Like clockwork, he started to have a drink at 5:00 p.m. every day, when before, he would only drink on weekends or during visits with friends. If we were not going to be home at that time, he would plan ahead and pack a small cooler with ice, liquor, and 7UP. If I questioned his need for a drink, he would explain how it relaxed him.

Dr. M. returned and handed us a schedule with two appointments. "I would like you to return in a few weeks for a follow-up visit to review the results of the tests," he said as he handed Val a release form to sign for his medical records from his primary care physician. Val hesitated for a few moments, then signed.

"Val, I encourage you to drink less alcohol," Dr. M. said.

Val nodded. "I will start to cut back."

"Good," the doctor said and gave a smile of encouragement. "It can cause more harm with ataxia and your apparent neuropathy."

Val said nothing.

We thanked Dr. M. for his time and left the exam room. We walked toward the elevator bank to make our way to the lab on the next floor down.

CHAPTER 3—TEST RESULTS

Two weeks passed after our initial visit to Mayo Clinic. Val had the MRI of his brain performed in Tucson and the results sent directly to Dr. M. We had an 8:00 a.m. appointment and left early for the drive to Phoenix. The temperature had already climbed higher than eighty degrees, and neighbors were out early, walking their dogs, as we drove through the neighborhood.

We arrived late, and I dropped Val off at the entrance, suggesting he go up to the third floor and check in while I park the car. He slowly got out of the car and steadied himself with the car door. As he found his balance with the aid of his cane, he gently shut the door, and I watched in the rearview mirror as he struggled to walk. I thought about how these appointments were a waste of time: he was never going to accept alcohol as the cause for his physical deterioration. A waste of time, definitely—but I still hoped.

I met him upstairs as he finished the patient check-in. We had been seated for less than ten minutes when the same young man from our first visit called us to the examination area. We followed him down the hallway and around the corner to a different exam room. Similar large chairs were in the room, and we sat in the same locations: Val next to the doctor's desk and I next to the door. A few minutes passed, and Dr. M. entered the room. He greeted us with a smile and shook our hands.

"How have you been doing, Val?" he asked.

"About the same," Val replied.

"All right, let's review your test results," Dr. M. said. "The clinical interpretation from your electromyography, or EMG, is peripheral neuropathy, and the MRI revealed a slight shrinking at the base of the brain, which supports the diagnosis of ataxia."

"Can the neuropathy and ataxia be reversed?"

"No, but you can slow down the progression. I believe the chief reason for your brain and neuropathic symptoms is alcohol."

Val stared at Dr. M. and offered no response.

Dr. M. continued, "Your primary care physician also believes it is alcohol."

Val shook his head.

"You need to wean yourself off alcohol. And for the pain, I want you to stop taking oxycodone; instead, I would like you to try gabapentin."

Val nodded and agreed to reduce his alcohol by half and then slowly to none. He halfheartedly agreed to consider joining a support group, perhaps Alcoholics Anonymous (AA). *Huh*, I thought, *he never joined AAA; he sure isn't going to join AA.* I smiled at my silly comparison because I knew Val would think he could do this himself. He never accepted anyone telling him what to do or not to do, and he always asserted he did not like group meetings. He could handle his problems by himself.

We stood up and both shook Dr. M.'s hand goodbye and thanked him. On our way out of the office, we stopped at the check-in desk and made a follow-up appointment for six months, but the earliest available appointment was almost seven months away, December 18, 2017, the day before Val's fifty-sixth birthday. Three months later, Val was admitted to the hospital and I was going to meet Charlie.

CHAPTER 4—CHARLIE

DAY 1 continued, and I was daydreaming in the hospital parking lot. The phone rang and brought me back to the moment. I shot a quick glance at the car clock and realized I had been sitting there for fifteen minutes. Val must be calling again to ask where I was and why I hadn't returned to the hospital.

I answered, "Hello?"

His animated voice, pitched higher than during the last call, asked, "Where are you?"

"I am in the parking lot and on my way to your room. I will be there in a few minutes."

With the excitement of a child, he squealed, "He is peeking his head out again and is winking at me. I say hello. He hides his face, then comes back out to see me."

"I will see you in a few minutes, and then you can show me." I hung up the phone and took a deep breath, turned off the car, and headed to the hospital's main entrance. Approaching the coffee shop, I stopped to buy a tall, skinny, sugar-free-vanilla latte. I was going to need some caffeine for my afternoon visit with Val, who was in acute care.

I paid for my coffee and took the elevator to the third floor. I walked to the entrance and pressed the large red button. The heavy double doors, standing stoic like the well-practiced Queen's Guard, slowly opened, and I slipped through before they finished swinging wide. I noticed that acute care and intensive care were together, in the same rectangular wing, with the nursing stations in the center facing out to all the patient rooms. The individual rooms were spacious, and oversized windows allowed ample sunlight and glimpses of the mountains.

Val was in room 444, the last room on the left. I turned left and headed toward his room, took a deep breath, and entered through the drawn curtain. Val was sitting in a large chair beside the bed, a yellow-and-white gown draped loosely around his swollen abdomen and a soft white blanket covering his lap. An IV had been inserted into his left hand and an oxygen saturation monitor was attached to a left finger. Several lines of fluid were making their journey down the intravenous tube and into his bloodstream. His cheeks were rosy and his blue eyes were gleaming; it was how he looked after his first alcoholic drink.

He glanced up at me as I entered the room. Moving around the large chair to stand behind him, I leaned over and kissed his forehead in the same fashion a parent would kiss their child. He looked pensive, pulled the blanket up to his chin, and held it there, a guileless child snuggling in a favorite blanket.

He glanced toward the nurses' station to check for people and then said sheepishly, "It isn't very private in here."

Puzzled, I said, "What do you mean?"

"To have sex. We can't do that now, not here," he replied with a forbidding voice.

I started to ask what made him think I wanted to have sex but then stopped myself from asking a ridiculous question, stopped trying to rationalize with an irrational person. Though I pondered his comment for a minute and found it curious he would think about sex, I concluded that sexuality was deep within his psyche, as he often exhibited sexual thoughts and vulgarity. He frequently embarrassed me with his sexual comments to friends at dinner parties and other outings, thinking he was charming and clever, when most women were stupefied or disgusted by his remarks. I thought, *Alcoholics often embarrass and humiliate their friends, family, and loved ones.*

I held my hand out to take his hand and replied, "I wasn't planning on having sex." Changing the subject, I inquired, "Tell me, how are you feeling?"

He smiled and pointed to the cabinet along the wall his bed faced. "See, there it is!" he said excitedly.

"There what is?" I asked with a probing expression.

"The puppy," he said, continuing to point to the cabinet.

As he stretched his pointed finger as far as he could reach, several questions scrolled through my mind: *Do I turn to where he is pointing and agree I see the puppy? Do I turn toward the cabinet and tell him I don't see anything but a cabinet and medical supplies? Or do I stand still and ask if he is experiencing alcohol withdrawal and hallucinations?*

Oh crap, I can no longer pretend—we have been pretending about too much in our marriage, and for too long.

I turned toward the cabinet, and without hesitation, I blurted, "Val, there is nothing there. I don't see the puppy."

He became agitated and snapped, "Look! It is right there! See, he just peeked his head out again and winked."

I repeated that I did not see anything. I thought, *What do I say next? I don't know how to respond to someone who is hallucinating. Do I explain what is happening to him?* As I pondered that question, I realized I had never known how to communicate with an alcoholic—how to respond during his fits of blaming, self-pity, and arrogance. I gazed down the hallway to see if a nurse was nearby. I wondered if the nurses had visited with him during his hallucinations and if they could help me cope with Val's entry into the confusing and the blurry mental state of alcohol withdrawal.

Uneasy with my thoughts, I grasped at ideas to change the subject. Turning to look at Val, I reached my right hand down to the chair arm and slowly slumped down in the bright turquoise visitor's chair. I was wiggling in the chair to get comfortable when Val exclaimed, "You sat on Charlie!"

"Who is Charlie?"

"He is the little boy. You are sitting on him!" He gasped with wild eyes focused on me, straining to understand how it was possible I could not see Charlie.

"Oh. I didn't realize I was sitting on him." I stood up and told Val I did not see Charlie. I was at a loss for words. Puppies and a boy named Charlie. What was next?

"I need a glass of water," I said as I turned to the corridor and stepped out of the room. I found one of the nurses behind the monitoring desk. I glanced at her name tag—Sharon—then I looked up and was intrigued by her striking resemblance to me, although much younger. I introduced myself and asked for a minute of her time. She gave me a gentle smile and a look of kindness and empathy. I told her Val was seeing a puppy and asked if she had noticed he was hallucinating. She nodded and explained he had been conjuring up visions for several hours.

"We have upgraded him from acute care to intensive care. We started him on Ativan. It is used to treat anxiety and drug withdrawal," Sharon said. Then she calmly asked, "How much does he drink each day?"

No fooling the nurses. They must see this all the time with patients who come in for medical help but don't disclose that they depend on alcohol— probably unaware that they are going to go into withdrawals within twenty-four hours or slightly longer. In a soft voice, I answered, "He drinks two exceptionally large glasses of Canadian Club and 7UP every night. He uses fifteen to twenty ounces of whiskey." I was embarrassed to tell Sharon how much he drank. But then I asked myself a question: *Why am I embarrassed? I am not the person drinking a half gallon of whiskey every three days. In fact, he is finally at a place where he can begin to get help.* Too often, embarrassment had been a part of my life with an alcoholic. Embarrassment became a frequent visitor at my guesthouse—especially when Val and I socialized with friends or family.

Having heard this story many times, she didn't hesitate to respond, "Honey, you are in for a long, tough road. This is just the beginning of recovery. For most, it's the beginning of many false starts and failures."

My eyes widened and tears pooled in the corners, and I muttered, "A long, tough road? I have been on this long road for the last twenty-five years, each year getting worse. I have to endure more?" I knew I could no longer live with an alcoholic. My love and compassion for Val had faded—no, almost vanished. And if he failed in rehabilitation, I would lose my self-control and everything I had ever felt for him.

In a soft voice, I asked, "Sharon, how should I respond to Val when he tells me about a hallucination?"

She replied, "You do not tell him you see the hallucination or agree with one he shares with you. Explain that he is hallucinating because he has stopped drinking and that these hallucinations will pass."

"How long will his hallucinations last?"

"Alcohol withdrawal affects everyone differently. Withdrawal symptoms are usually worse on the second or third day after the last drink and will take as little as a week. Generally, the more one drank, the more frequently one drank, and the longer someone was an alcoholic, the higher the chances of experiencing severe alcohol withdrawal symptoms. Some people become quiet and sleep through most of the withdrawal process. Other people get agitated, sleep little, and fight the entire withdrawal period."

Sharon paused for a moment, softly laughed, then said, "I worked at another hospital, and once I had a nun for a patient; she was hospitalized for heart issues and went through withdrawals. She cursed like the best of the salty old sailors. And when the church's minister visited her, she flirted—telling him she was getting old and wanted to have sex before she died.

"Honey," she said to me, "the withdrawal process is unpredictable, but just remember, your husband will not be himself, and, most likely, he won't remember anything."

Crap. My husband is not going to be the patient who sleeps through his withdrawal period, and once he realizes no one else sees his hallucinations, he is going to get agitated. I knew my husband. He was going to be like the nun. I couldn't possibly have known, but would later discover, that he was going to be far worse than the nun, with the deepest, ugliest parts of his personality unleashed by the ravages of alcoholism.

I slowly turned around and walked back to his room. Room 444. Val was staring at the sliding-glass-door entrance, waiting for me to return. His monitoring of my actions gave me a chill as I recalled the years I had spent being monitored: my time—what time was I leaving, where was I going, and when would I return—always observed, and an interrogation ensued when a late return was not announced with a notification call because, well, that was just inconsiderate to not let him know I would be casually late.

I was reflecting on how his probing dull eyes made me angry as I pulled back the curtain, took a deep breath, and stepped through the doorway. Val greeted me with a suspicious glare, and he snapped, "You told on me, didn't you? You told them about the puppy and Charlie? Why don't you mind your own business?"

I exhaled the breath I had been holding. The next several days were going to be like walking into a blizzard wearing only my flip-flops, shorts, and a T-shirt!

"I didn't tattle to the nurse. I asked if she knew about the puppy and Charlie. She told me she knew about the hallucinations and to tell you they are not real; they are part of the alcohol withdrawal—"

Val cut in, "The puppy is right there. I am not seeing things."

He sat back in his chair, glaring harder and clenching his teeth. "You can go home. You never back me up. You never support me. You always agree with the doctors. I don't want you here."

I stood and stared at him, and I felt rejuvenated and strong; his behavior no longer mattered to me. His cold stares and heartless words no longer hurt me. How many times had he tried to hurt me with words? Hundreds? Thousands? Avoiding the need to deal with his emotional issues—the causes of his relief drinking and eventual alcoholism—he used words like poison-tipped darts, hurling them at my eyes every time he felt misunderstood, insecure, or fearful. Yes. Yes, I was done being hurt. I had walked alongside an alcoholic on his journey to chronic alcoholism, sharing in every emotion and drama possible, but I was done tolerating the impact it had had on my life. I was ready to change my pathway.

I didn't respond to his demand to leave. I was ready to leave. I gently pulled his blanket up over his lap and told him to rest and that I would see him tomorrow morning.

CHAPTER 5—NOT MY FAULT

I arrived home from the hospital and thought about my first visit to the ICU: Charlie and the puppy—what did they look like in Val's mind; Sharon asking me how much Val drank each day and telling me I had a long road ahead; recalling the feeling of heaviness in the bottom of my gut—a sick feeling; and Val, even in alcohol withdrawal, revealing those deep, dark wounds of insecurity as he repeated tired, trite phrases of "never supporting me" and "never backing me up," struggling to gain my concurrence. I felt numb as I sat in the dark, my mind now wandering back to the beginning of his love affair with alcohol, back to when Val started drinking every day.

We began our life together after college graduation, and in our early years, daily consumption was not an option given our meager take-home pay. We drank socially on weekends when we were in our twenties. He didn't suddenly make a giant leap from drinking socially on weekends to drinking daily. There must have been a sign. *What did I miss? When did his drinking escalate?* I thought about our wedding and how much alcohol he had consumed that day—enough to pass out in the hotel bathroom and sleep in the fetal position next to the toilet. He was thirty.

Following our wedding in 1992, I traveled for business for several years, often two, sometimes three, weeks a month, leaving Sunday mornings and returning Friday evenings. Val certainly had time to carouse and drink while I was away on business trips. Then it dawned on me when he must have begun drinking on weekdays all the while continuing his behavior of socially drinking with me on weekends.

It was shortly after our wedding. It was a cold, rainy winter day in

Seattle, Washington, and I had the usual winter crud—but worse than usual. I visited my doctor, and during the exam, she confirmed that I had an extreme case of viral pneumonia. She immediately admitted me to the hospital. I called Val on my way to check in and asked him to bring my toothbrush, hairbrush, and a change of clothes. He agreed and assured me that he would go to the hospital after work.

He arrived at the hospital after dinner, around 7:00. He walked in, came to my bed, and gave me a big hug. We visited for about forty-five minutes, and then he said he had to go home and work but would return the next evening. I was exhausted from struggling to breathe and needed rest. He kissed me goodbye and left.

The next evening, he arrived again at 7:00. This time he brought our friend Matt—the best man in our wedding. They visited for an hour and then told me they were going out for a few drinks. I was annoyed that I was in the hospital and he was staying for just an hour and then leaving with his best buddy. I thought, *They could have stayed and visited longer. They could have played a game or watched television with me.* I did not say anything—I was tired and needed to rest. Val kissed me goodbye and said he would be back tomorrow evening.

Later that night, I awakened, and something did not feel right. I woke up feeling disturbed and worried about the dogs at home. Although they had a dog door for access to the yard and were probably fine home alone, I still felt anxious. I called the home telephone (before everyone owned mobile phones), but no one answered. We had a phone on the nightstand next to my side of the bed. The fact that Val had not answered implied the obvious—he wasn't home. I assumed that he and Matt were barhopping.

The next evening, Val arrived at the hospital at the same time. I asked him if he had gone out last night, and he said no. I told him I had called but he had not answered. He explained that he had been working in the living room and had fallen asleep. I didn't believe him, but it was futile to probe, and, frankly, I didn't have the energy. He stayed for a few hours, and he watched television as I drifted in and out of sleep. When a nurse arrived to draw my blood, as one did every few hours, Val stood up and kissed me good night.

I spent four nights in the hospital. On the last night, he arrived at the usual time—7:00. He stayed for less than an hour and then told me he was going to visit Matt. When Val and Matt did not go to local haunts for a drink, Val would go to the Olympic Hotel, where Matt was the food and beverage manager. I thought, *Of course you are going to see Matt. Another night out with free drinks and dinner from Matt. How often do you visit Matt when I am traveling for business?*

I knew Val and Matt considered themselves attractive men, and Val, on more than one occasion, would tell me how women would ask them to dance, and when they declined, women would sourly respond by telling Val and Matt they were pretty boys. Val would emphasize that some women told him he was more attractive than Matt. I never reacted to Val telling me those stories. I understood that his good looks made him feel secure and confident. I consciously uplifted his self-confidence—I wanted him to feel good about himself and be happy.

Val hanging out with his drinking buddy may have been the only thing that gave him confidence, but tonight, this behavior was unacceptable. I was unhappy that he was not staying with me. I expected more compassion and attention while being confined in the hospital. His behavior disappointed me, and decades later, I would find it crushing me, taking the air out of my lungs, and pressing all its weight onto my empty chest. He would suck the life out of me with his insecurities, false pride, and addiction.

I was released the next day, and Val picked me up after work and took me home. I could barely walk up the stairs to the second floor—the main living area in our home. He held my arm, and together, one step at a time, we made our way up the curved staircase. He tucked me into bed and joined me—watching a movie until I fell asleep. He was so patient, kind, and attentive that evening.

I stayed home from work for the next week. It was awfully hard for me to breathe and was a struggle just to move between the bedroom and kitchen. My inhaler helped, but I was slow to get well. That week Val went out one evening, desiring something other than watching me sleep or slowly shuffle from one sitting area to the next. He was going out with Matt, and he said he would be home around midnight. At 1:00 a.m., I suddenly woke, and he was standing next to me. I shot upright in bed, my heart pounding. "Jesus, you scared me!" I said.

"I'm sorry; I didn't mean to startle you," he quietly replied, as though others around us were still asleep.

"Something happened tonight," he said.

"What?"

"I was crossing some train tracks and hit a high spot on the track. I'm sorry—I wrecked your car."

"You what?" I gasped and then started coughing because I could not get enough oxygen. "Why were you driving my car?"

He did not answer my question but continued, "The tracks were uneven, and I think the front axle broke when I hit them."

"I thought you went out with Matt. Where are the train tracks?"

"We went to Tacoma, and I took a shortcut home through the commercial area where the train tracks traverse. I am not familiar with the area in the dark and hit the tracks going too fast."

"I work in Tacoma, and I know that going through the commercial area is not faster than taking the interstate to drive home. Why were you near that part of town? It is the seedy part of town."

"Matt and I were downtown. I thought it would be a shortcut."

Not believing him, I said nothing. I had no way of knowing where he had been or with whom. It was the first time in our marriage I knew he was lying—he had totaled my car and broken my trust; I awoke to the subtle changes in his behavior and drinking.

No significant changes occurred in the next few years. We moved from Seattle to an island north of Seattle, where we lived in a charming lakeside home. He was passionate about the small mail-order water-sports business he managed, immersing himself in the daily process. He worked tirelessly as a one-man show, and he thrived at being independent, creative, and productive. Meanwhile, I started my own telecommunications consulting practice, and together, we were on our way to sharing the personal fulfillment of self-employment.

Unfortunately, Val's business dwindled, and we made the painful decision to close the business. Val was disappointed, and the closure was clearly a major life stressor, resulting in a cascade of negative thoughts and inactivity. As my consulting practice demanded my full attention and significant traveling, he was left home, alone, to focus on his personal losses and what he perceived to be my personal gains, although I included him on projects when possible and never alienated him by referring to the consulting practice as mine. The more he wallowed in disappointment and self-pity, the more he begrudged my career. He felt ashamed he did not have a profession and could not command my salary. He would tell me that I thought less of him as a man because he couldn't possibly earn my pay. I assured him that was not true, and I encouraged him to look for work on the sole criterion of how satisfied it made him, not based on how much money he could earn.

He struggled. I left him alone week after week as my travels consumed my time, only to see him on weekends. He was isolated on the island, with few friends or nearby neighbors. When home on the weekends, I saw liquor bottles in the trash can, and it was obvious he was drinking while I was away on weekdays as well as drinking on the weekends when I was home. Heck, he didn't try to hide it. He openly made his evening drinks, unabashed that he drank every night with his favorite sixteen-ounce pink plastic cup he dubbed his "sippy cup."

One Friday night, after taking the last ferryboat across the bay, I walked across the passenger pickup lot, through mud puddles and misty rain, to find him waiting in the car—engine running and music playing on the radio. I flung my luggage and briefcase in the back seat and plopped down in the front seat, exhausted from the East Coast to West Coast jaunt. I glanced at him, and his head was turned to face out his window. He took a moment and then wrenched his face away from the window and toward me. "There is something I have to tell you," he said.

"What?" I asked.

He hesitated, as though to build courage. "I got a DUI while you were in Ohio, and I spent the night in jail."

I blankly stared at him—I showed no expression of anger or disappointment, though I was extremely disappointed. I continued to look straight into his eyes, my eyes begging him to tell me more. He continued with an elaborate story of how he hadn't been drunk, but after he had left the restaurant, the police had entrapped him as he had pulled out onto the highway. He told me how their Breathalyzer machine hadn't been operative, and they had directed him to perform a field sobriety test.

I sat and listened as he explained how he had said the alphabet, and when he'd finished with *X*, *Y*, and *Z*, the police officer had said he was wrong.

He hesitated and then continued, telling me about the evening in his jail cell and how the next day when he had returned to his car, he had discovered that twenty dollars was missing from his center console. As he finished his reenactment of the evening, I sat looking at him but barely hearing his voice. I realized he was fabricating his story to appear as though he had done nothing wrong and the police were unjustified, if not actually corrupt, in arresting him. I thought, *What a tale he is weaving. An embellished story to cover his drinking, to cover up the seriousness behind his first DUI. What happens next?* I was disappointed with his behavior and, yes, angry with him and his lack of self-control and lack of awareness that his behavior impacted both of us. And yet, I did nothing. I enabled his behavior. I was the ultimate caregiver and "helper" and had been since my formative years.

I understood at that moment that Val had had a lifestyle change, and I was seeing the presence of his addictive personality: the need to drink daily. He used alcohol to numb his emotional pain and avoid dealing with the causes underlying his pain. His addiction resulted in mood swings, defensiveness, and sometimes irrational thinking—which I would later learn was *emotional* thinking because addiction is not rational behavior. What I didn't understand then and wouldn't fully grasp until years later—because I experienced a pattern of behavior that repeated—is the alcoholic's self-determination (or more accurately stated, the addictive personality's self-preservation) and use of cunning and manipulative tactics to secure family members' willingness to agree or help them. Once that help is secured, the alcoholic uses their innate ability to take little or no responsibility for their actions, often deflecting or blaming. How Val presented the DUI to me, blaming the police and taking no responsibility for his drinking and driving, was one of many examples of his addictive personality's self-preservation—deflecting and blaming.

Learning of the DUI was also the moment I firmly established myself in playing the role of a family member of an alcoholic—and making the mistake of using rational behavior to relate to the emotional behavior of the alcoholic: trying to fix or improve the alcoholic's life choices. Much later in life, I would learn that my role in our relationship was as a "codependent." Melody Beattie writes, "A codependent person is one who has let another person's behavior affect him or her, and who is obsessed with controlling that person's behavior."[2] And

2. Beattie, *Codependent No More*, 34.

codependency is a concept that attempts to characterize imbalanced relationships where one person enables another person's self-destructive tendencies (such as addiction, poor mental health, immaturity, irresponsibility, or under-achievement).[3] I was a codependent and an enabler. And later, when I learned these terms, I also learned that I had codependency characteristics long before Val got his DUI—I had those characteristics in my childhood and the first day I met Val.

I did not understand alcoholism, and I did not have the communication skills to relate to the alcoholic, especially in the early stage when behavior changes are infrequent and subtle. I subsequently learned in Al-Anon literature about detachment, that when living with an alcoholic, there is a guideline of Do Nots (figure 2):

- Do Not cover up for another's mistakes or misdeeds.
- Do Not manipulate situations so others will eat, go to bed, get up, pay bills, not drink, or behave as we see fit.
- Do Not suffer because of the actions or reactions of other people.
- Do Not allow ourselves to be used or abused by others in the interest of another's recovery.
- Do Not create a crisis.
- Do Not push anyone but yourself.
- Do Not disallow the alcoholic to experience the consequences of their own actions.
- Do not do for others what they can do for themselves.[4]

I spent decades in a relationship with an alcoholic, and I never took the time to research and learn about alcoholism, to learn about the addictive personality, or to learn about myself as a partner with an alcoholic. It wasn't until after Val's admission to the ICU that I researched alcoholism and learned of its four stages: Pre-Alcoholic, Prodromal (Early Alcoholic), Crucial (Middle Alcoholic), and Chronic (Late Alcoholic)[5]. I could identify the alcoholic's behavioral changes in the four stages of alcoholism (figure 3), and I started to identify the behavioral changes in my life PATH with the alcoholic—something

3. "Codependency," BPDFamily.com.
4. "Detachment," Al-Anon website.
5. Sweisgood, "Understanding the Progression of Alcoholism."

I was not expecting but found valuable. In fact, understanding my behavior would be essential to acknowledging and accepting my reality, my circumstances. Only then could I begin to make appropriate changes: to live and be responsible for my own life and allow Val to live and be responsible for his.

Val's DUI supported the behavioral changes in the Early Alcoholic stage: levels of consumption escalating with an urgency for the first drink (gulping the first drink), drinking bolstered by excuses, feelings of guilt, and lying about drinking or events involving drinking.

And not surprisingly, changes in my behavior reflected the various stages of his alcoholism. In the Early Alcoholic stage, I hid from family and friends the fact that he had driven alone to a bar and had gotten intoxicated, subsequently getting a DUI. I told him to drink less, although he was unable to discuss his problem, or admit he had a problem, and he was unable to share his guilt.

But what are my phases? I am aware of my behavior changes in each of Val's alcoholic stages, but to my knowledge, there are no clinical phases for a person involved with an alcoholic. The acronym PATH helps me label my phases with an alcoholic. I was on a PATH with Val. We began with Partnership, a healthy relationship with my best friend: sharing, loving, and co-creating a life together. Partnership led to Anger as Val became immersed in the Crucial stage of alcoholism. Anger turned to Tolerance, a mechanism to cope with the alcoholic, suppressing my feelings and giving up and giving in. But not all was lost, because I learned to detach myself from the alcoholic, and with restorative steps, I started Healing.

After Val's DUI, I felt I had one foot in the Partnership phase of my PATH, still being kind and grateful and enjoying my moments with Val, but the other foot was stepping into the Anger phase, covering for his actions and taking more responsibility for the "shared" life.

Walk with me through the remaining chapters, read my stories, and witness the stages of alcoholism and my journey down the PATH as a codependent. Will any of these stories resonate with your personal life experiences?

CHAPTER 6—AGAINST HIS WILL

DAY 2. I tossed and turned through the night, waking often from vivid dreams of Val hallucinating and having temper tantrums—certain these were occurring while I was away, and yet the nurses never corroborated these fears. I imagined what his body and mind were experiencing as they struggled to cope without alcohol. Exhausted, I needed to sleep but, instead, turned to my side and rolled out of bed. I lifted my dog, Brandy, off the bed and set her on the cool tile floor. We both stretched, her back legs extended straight and my arms up over my head. I yawned, and we walked to the kitchen. I started the coffee maker, took her dog food pail from the cupboard, and added kibble to her bowl, her ears perking up as she heard the pings of the kibble landing on the bottom. As I placed her bowl on the floor, I watched as she sniffed the kibble and slowly nibbled her food. She was sullen and ate slowly; perhaps she sensed my anxiety and concern.

That day's work schedule was light, taking only half a day, which was fortunate, as I struggled to concentrate. After work and a quick lunch, I drove to the hospital. I walked into the ICU and walked toward room 444. Muffled voices were coming from behind the curtain—one voice much louder than the other—maybe one of Val's doctors? I slid the right curtain panel open and slipped inside the room. The lead doctor of the ICU team of caregivers, referred to as the intensivist, and a nurse were in the room. Val was asleep. The intensivist, a tall, slender man in his early sixties, glanced up at me and stopped talking. He smiled, extended his hand, and gave me a firm handshake.

"Your husband is a very sick man," he said to me in a direct but professional manner. "His magnesium is extremely low, and he isn't able to hold sustainable oxygen on his own. He is in a life-or-death situation."

I thought, *I knew alcohol was causing physical and mental damage to his body, but, honestly, I did not know he was in a life-or-death situation. His drinking has ravaged his body.* I felt compassion for him, and yet I was upset he had done this to himself. I felt I could no longer help him, nor should I help him, because he wasn't helping himself.

A few months prior, he had claimed he was dying—he could feel it. It was an early summer evening, and I checked on him before bed, like I always did. He was sitting on the edge of the bed, his legs hanging over the side, head down, looking into his lap—he had a gun in his hand. He had become increasingly despondent after his Mayo Clinic appointments. He may have had the courage to end his life that night, but I took the gun away and told him he wasn't going to die, not tonight, and not with a gun.

The intensivist continued, "We will continue to treat his heart and keep an oxygen mask on him as well as continue to treat his edema. Val is sleeping after being sedated."

"Did you sedate him because of the alcohol withdrawal symptoms, including his hallucinations?" I asked quietly, hoping not to wake Val.

"No," he replied stoically. "We sedated him because he became agitated when he realized we would not let him leave the hospital. He kept trying to pull the IV out of his arm and get out of bed. We had to prevent him from harming himself or the staff."

I looked away from the intensivist and toward Val—stiffening my body and stopping my breath—as my eyes scanned the Velcro-strapped restraints around each wrist and tethered to the bed. I moved my eyes down the blanket covering his legs and saw the ankle restraints—tethered to the bed frame just like the wrist straps. The restraint straps were long enough to give him some movement, but he was a prisoner to the bed. I understood that the restraints were necessary, and it saddened me.

I thanked the intensivist for the information. He told me to hang in there, intending to assure me. He left the room, and I watched him continue down the hallway, I presumed visiting the other ICU patients. The nurse stayed in the room, and he said, "Val is having a terrible reaction to detox. He is going to have an exceedingly difficult time here, and rehabilitation will be difficult too. Perhaps you should go home and get some rest. He will probably wake up early this evening, and you can try to visit again."

"All right," I said. As I looked at Val, a wave of sadness bathed my face. He was asleep, but his face was tense and his eyebrows were slightly scrunched. He did not have a relaxed and serene look of slumber. I sensed his mind was not at peace, even though he was sedated. I glanced a moment longer, then turned away and left his room. A tear came to my eye as I walked down the hall and out through the Queen's Guard.

I drove home and sat on the couch. I felt empty and numb. My thoughts were fuzzy. I took a two-hour nap and woke in time to feed Brandy and take her for an early evening walk. Brandy and I walked up our street, passing the usual neighbors that walked their dogs during the same hour. The dog walkers always greeted each other and visited for a few minutes, letting the dogs touch noses and sniff one another. Taking methodical steps, I was sullen and reluctant to smile and visit with any neighbor. How could I share with my neighbors that Val was in the hospital, strapped to his bed and hallucinating?

Shame crept into my stomach and rolled into a ball, my gut warning of nausea. Uttering the word "alcoholism" to a close friend or family member was unthinkable. Covering up his undeniable will to drink was safer than the consequence of exposing our personal hell. It was safer to avoid explaining an irrational life to a rational person. I was in the Tolerance phase on my PATH—unhappy and coping to survive. I wasn't confronting the devil in my personal hell, and I was stuck on my PATH. I needed to move along my PATH. I needed to take a path that was best for me. But it was easier to live alone in the darkness of my personal hell. After all, I could certainly manage it—dodge the darts thrown at me and handle the day-to-day tasks. I had been doing that for years. But I wasn't safe, and I was joyless and simply enduring my life. I allowed these visitors of shame and joylessness to visit my guesthouse and stay too long.

No, keep walking. Keep your head down. Then I heard a familiar voice behind me say, "Hey, how is it going?" It was my next-door neighbor, Leigh, who always says "hey" instead of "hello." She is a true Southern girl from Florida and has charming mannerisms and a soft

Southern accent.

I turned to see Leigh approaching, her white flopping hat waving in the warm evening breeze, her soft, highlighted strawberry-red hair dancing around her face. Exhaling a sigh of relief, I replied, "Hey. I am taking one day at a time." One day at a time, and on Day 2, it felt like a week had passed. I wondered if I could confide in Leigh and share my story—be raw and honest. Yes, I could. I could trust her to be objective and nonjudgmental. She understood my world with Val's lies, self-pity, and selfishness, for she had once been married to an alcoholic—the father of her children—and her two sisters were both alcoholics; she knew too well the strife of alcoholism. Yes, I could sit with her and let the stories leave their dark hiding place and dance off my lips, one at a time, elated with their escape. Maybe she would share some of her stories, offering me a glimpse of how she had dealt with alcoholics and had found a PATH that offered her peace and harmony—how she had found herself and had made it a priority to not let an alcoholic consume her. Yes, I wanted to share. I was ready to share.

"What do you mean you are taking it one day at a time? What is going on?" she asked.

I directed Brandy with a gentle tug to turn, and together, we walked toward Leigh. "Do you mind if we walk awhile with you?" I asked.

"Of course not," she said, raising her eyebrows and giving me an inquisitive look.

We walked slowly, and I recited the events leading to the trip to the ER, Val's admission to the ICU, and how I met Charlie. Leigh whipped her head around. "What? You sent shivers down my spine. Val is in a bad way right now!"

"Really bad."

She stared at me for a few minutes, a pensive, unblinking stare. "Tell me about how you and Val met and how long it took him to get to this point of crisis."

I smiled and responded, "It is a long story, a very long story." I started by telling her I had grown up in Washington. When I was in grade seven, my junior high school closed, and the following year, my neighbors and I were bused to College Place Junior High. The first day of school was like most for new kids—we were the newbies, the strangers. The local kids had grown up together starting in kindergarten, forming their various groups of friends in elementary school—long before any of us arrived from Edmonds Junior High. They grew up with each other, playing kick the can, hide-and-seek, and street ball games and swimming in pools. They played all summer long in their parents' backyards.

We were scattered throughout all the various classrooms, and it didn't take long to make friends with the local kids. I had the usual mix of eighth-grade classes—history, math, English, art, home economics, and science. Mrs. Parsons was my eighth-grade science teacher. She was a short, stout, middle-aged woman with a round face and warm smile. She had long blonde hair and wore it in an updo. She was very friendly and quite passionate about science—she made a special effort to greet the new kids, and then she assigned us to a lab desk with a local kid. I was assigned a lab desk with John. I sat on the right side and John sat on the left. The lab desk in front of us had two boys who were obviously good friends. They talked and laughed, confident in their strong friendship.

Those two boys were Val and Gordy. Val would tilt his head back just enough to sneak a glance at me, and when I caught him, he would quickly turn his head to face his lab desk. We exchanged these innocent glances for several weeks until one day I invited Val to go skiing with my parents and me. He agreed, and we saw each other for about three weeks, a lifetime in eighth grade, and then we decided to not like each other.

After graduating from ninth grade, we went to different high schools. I made new friends, dated other boys, and had no thoughts of Val since starting high school, until a year later, in eleventh grade, when we saw each other at a high school party. After the party, we resumed seeing each other on the weekends since we attended different high schools and both of us played sports after school. We spent our weekends sharing sport stories and what our zany friends had done that week in school. But more importantly, we shared our home life.

As a young child, I spent a great deal of time alone. I was an only child, and both of my parents worked. I spent many weekends with my grandmother—we would go bowling and out for lunch, and in the evening, as we watched *Lawrence Welk*, we sang and danced with the show's dancers. And after dancing in her living room, Grandma would tuck me into the bed that had slippery creamy white silk sheets, and she would sit beside me and read from a book—usually one of the Nancy Drew mystery stories. I liked spending weekends with Grandma. My parents cherished their weekends together; they were still young adults trying to manage work and raise a child after becoming parents at age seventeen.

When I didn't spend weekends with Grandma, my parents would take me to their boating friends' homes for dinner. Afterward, I would watch television with the other kids, and the parents would drink, smoke, and tell tall tales of their weekend boating adventures. I longed for more time with my parents—just the three of us.

In tenth grade, my world dramatically changed. My father was investigated by the Internal Revenue Service and was found guilty of tax fraud, resulting in minimum security prison time. While he was incarcerated, my mother took Valium and other pills to cope with my father's absence. I was sixteen, and I blossomed into my role of being codependent with my parents. I helped my mother with daily chores, making dinner, and ensuring she awoke from her pill-induced naps. I learned I had to rely on myself and cover up my feelings and needs. I never shared my family life with school friends, Grandma, or other relatives. I lived with my sadness and the shame that started with my father's troubles, keeping family stories tucked away, deep inside, not sharing with a single soul until Val. He became my conduit for secrets and my best friend. Shame and embarrassment visited my guesthouse long before I was married to an alcoholic—these visitors taught me to give in and give up, to tolerate. And sometimes, instead of tolerating, I acted out and behaved badly. I experienced Anger and Tolerance on my childhood PATH, and I repeated those experiences on my PATH with an alcoholic husband.

Val eagerly shared his home life with me. Val's father was a recovering alcoholic and had been sober for years before we met. And his father had a dark side—he belittled his wife and his children. Those four boys could never do anything right. When Val shared his passion to become an architect, his father denigrated him, saying, "There are too many architects and you wouldn't be as good." The time Val asked to go to a downhill skiing camp, his father degradingly explained, "Competitive skiers are born only in Europe and train in Europe—you could never be competitive. It is a waste of money." One belittling comment after another slowly eroded Val's self-confidence and interest in being with his family. I was loving and supportive—my self-confidence blossomed over the years. In turn, he gave me companionship, attention, and the unconditional love I needed. At least I thought it was unconditional love.

The summer before my senior year in high school, my father returned home from McNeil Island Federal Penitentiary. He had secured a job as a taxi driver during his stay in a halfway house, which he continued, doing an evening shift once permanently back home. One afternoon I walked to the backyard and found my father sunbathing in his tighty-whities. He was extremely tan and in good shape due to his relaxed stay in a minimum security prison. I said, "Geez, Dad, put a bathing suit on."

He responded, "My underwear is fine. No one can see me."

"Will you take me to a party tonight and pick me up at midnight? My truck doesn't always start."

"You don't need to go to a party tonight. Besides, you work in the morning."

"Don't tell me what to do!"

"Don't you talk back to me: I am still your father."

"You lost that privilege when you went to prison. You told me I couldn't tell anyone where you were, and I had to lie. Mom and I told friends you were fishing in Alaska, and everyone knew we were lying. I am so embarrassed that I lied for you."

"Now listen here, young lady; you will respect me and not talk back."

"No, Dad, you lost my respect. You lost my respect when you committed fraud and left me and mom alone. She couldn't handle the situation, and she took prescription pills to compensate for her fears and sadness. I bet she didn't tell you how one night I couldn't find her in the house. I panicked that something had happened in her pill-popping stupor and began to call friends, the police, and the hospital. No one had seen her.

"I was making those phone calls sitting on the edge of your bed when something caused me to look between the pillows and the wall. And there she lay—wedged between the bed and wall. She had passed out from taking too many pills.

"I had to be responsible and help Mom cope with your absence. Dad, you don't get to tell me you are my father, and you don't get to tell me what I can and can't do—not anymore."

My relationship with my father soured. We barely spoke. Later that year, my senior year in high school, Val and I decided to move away from our parents' homes and live together—we thought we would be happier together. We rented a small one-bedroom apartment in the spring. I worked at Sears, making collections calls at night, and he worked for a construction company. I graduated from high school, and Val passed the GED test for his high school certification. We spent the rest of the summer together in our modest, barely furnished apartment. We worked full-time in the summer and yet never had any money. After paying rent, we had a few dollars each week to spend on food. I remember grocery shopping and adding up the price of each item as we placed it in our cart. Our refrigerator was bare except for Kool-Aid, eggs, milk, bacon, and Wonder Bread. Val's mom would occasionally bring over a fresh salmon they had caught fishing off the Edmonds shoreline or something she baked—usually chocolate cake, Val's favorite. She made the best chocolate cake!

We struggled and we were poor. I knew I was going to go to college and our time living together was temporary. After high school graduation, I went to college. Val followed, and we attended the same college for a year. Then he left school and went back to Edmonds, where he attended community college and worked delivering furniture.

We continued to see each other throughout my college years, except for the last six months. I knew Val was never going to finish college and had little aspiration to be successful. But, after my college graduation, we picked up where we left off—I guess I was not ready to start a new career and live in the city alone, still feeling that childhood loneliness that lived deep inside all those years. I found comfort in knowing Val was still attracted to me.

We rented a small, one-bedroom apartment barely large enough for furnishings: a small couch, one chair, one tall lamp, and a square dining table with four rickety chairs. We both had full-time jobs and two car payments, one student loan payment, and rent—we struggled, but we struggled together. And we grew together, our bond unbreakable.

I paused in my narrative with Leigh, wet my lips, and swallowed. I continued, explaining how we eventually saved enough money and bought our first home when we were twenty-eight, and we married two years later. I told her about Val's DUI and when I noticed he was drinking daily. And now, thirty-nine years after dating Val in eleventh grade and later marrying him, our bond, like a rope pulled too tight, had threads unravelling and breaking, losing strength.

Leigh stopped walking and gently touched my shoulder. I looked toward her, and she put her arms around me—giving me a gentle hug. Neither of us spoke for a minute, and then Leigh lifted her head and said, "It's not your fault. Val's drinking is not your fault or your responsibility."

"I know. But I enabled him to drink—made it easier for him to not do anything for himself. I helped him create work, and when he didn't work, I kept paying the bills, paying for his lifestyle, and buying him alcohol! He has never suffered the consequences of being an alcoholic, except for the deterioration of his health. I hate that word 'enabler,' but that is exactly what I am." I paused, swallowed hard, and continued, "I thought he would grow up and stop drinking, you know, realize he was wasting his life. It never dawned on me that he was irrational and I couldn't rationalize with him. We could never communicate as long as he was denying his drinking problem and I was denying he could stop without professional help."

Leigh nodded. Then she said, "When I was going through my divorce from an alcoholic, I read a book by Melody Beattie titled *Codependent No More: How to Stop Controlling Others and Start Caring for Yourself.* It is easy to read and explains a lot about codependents and the characteristics we—because I was a codependent and you are a codependent—have, often from an early age. Melody highlights caretaking, low self-worth, repression, obsession, controlling, denial, dependency, poor communication, weak boundaries, lack of trust, anger, and a few other characteristics. She then walks you through how to recognize those behaviors in yourself and what you must do to become aware of your behaviors, accept the behaviors, and then change the behaviors so you can learn to become un-dependent and take care of yourself. I may have a copy in the house. I will look for it and put it on your front doorstep."

"Thank you," I said.

We talked more, and Leigh comforted me, sharing stories about her ex-husband's drinking and her sister's DUI, which came with a high price tag of jail time, rehabilitation, and loss of driving privileges. When we arrived back at our driveways, she offered to take care of Brandy for a few hours while I went back to the hospital to visit Val and get an update from the nursing staff.

"Are you sure?" I said.

"Of course," she replied. "I insist. If you are later than ten, I will take Brandy back to your house."

"Thank you so much—Brandy will be happier with you than home alone."

I handed the leash to Leigh, gave Brandy an ear rub, and told her, "Goodbye. I am just going to the store, and I will be right back." I always told her I was going to the store, and she seemed to understand me. At least that is what we dog owners believe.

I turned away from Leigh's driveway, leapt over the rock drainage that divided the driveways, and got into my car. Backing down the driveway and out into the street, I began to envision Val in his hospital bed. Was he as sound asleep as he had been when I'd left him this afternoon, or was he awake and hallucinating? *I will know in fifteen minutes*, I told myself.

Precisely fifteen minutes later, I was in the hospital, reaching out to push the large red button, signaling the Queen's Guard to slowly open. I walked down the hallway and could hear several men's voices coming from Val's room. The men were patiently explaining something to Val. As I made my way to the curtain pulled across the sliding glass door, I heard Val arguing. I pulled back the curtain and saw two nurses, Paul and Tim, and the nurse's aide, Juan, surrounding Val's bed.

"You can't hold me here against my will," Val bellowed. "I have rights, and I am free to go home."

Val was thrashing his upper body around, trying to take the IV out of his left hand. Juan grabbed ahold of Val's right arm and restrained it. Paul, on the opposite side of the bed, was gripping Val's left arm while blocking the left hand from Val's attempt to pull out the IV. As Paul and Juan struggled to restrain Val, Tim was positioning the looped restraints around Val's wrists and strapping them into place.

Constraining his movements made Val angry.

"I have rights!" Val shouted. "You can't keep me here against my will. I need to go home and see my dog. Just give me ten minutes and I will come right back."

Tim replied calmly, "I can't let you go home. You have drugs in your body, and we are responsible for your safety. Besides, you need to get better. You are still in a touch and go situation."

Val jerked his shoulders and made a sudden move to raise his arms. He grew angrier as he looked at the restraints. He turned to me, his face a shade of rage, his eyes steel gray. Then he stared up into the face of Tim and demanded furiously, "Give me your radio. Give me your radio and your number now. I want to speak with your supervisor. You are holding me here against my will, and I am telling your supervisor."

The three men looked at me with the same question on their faces, What radio?

I explained that Val had spent the better part of the last year in pain and sitting all day and night watching television, mostly the police shows: *Law & Order, CSI, Law & Order: Special Victims Unit,* and *COPS.* In Val's mind, he was talking with police officers, and he wanted their dispatch radio and badge numbers. He intended to call dispatch and report the police officers for holding him against his will.

The three men nodded. All of us knew Val was confused, perhaps hallucinating. We could not rationalize with him, and all any of us could do was repeat why he was in the hospital and that he had to stay for several days. We explained that he had to stay while he detoxed and his heart condition improved. Tim explained to Val that he had drugs in his system and would for several days, and until his health improved, going home was not an option.

Val responded like a caged wildcat. He arched his back upward and tried swinging his arms, only to be defeated by the restraints. He hatched another plan and swung his legs sideways, attempting to land his feet on the floor. He kicked his right foot wildly across his left leg and back. Then he kicked his left leg outward and tried to reach Tim. He missed kicking Tim and tried again, stretching his body far out to the left. He continued to kick as Tim swiftly pulled up the side bed rails.

Hearing the commotion, another nurse, Dolly, rushed into the room to assist. She moved her hands forward and reached for Val's right foot. He thrashed right, and his foot made direct contact with Dolly's head. Dolly was about four feet ten inches tall and took the blow hard. She exploded backward and landed on her back. Bewildered, she wrapped her hand around the bed rail and rose on shaky legs. She clutched the bed rail for a few minutes, collecting herself. She was surprised; I was horrified!

"Are you all right?" I noticed that her forehead was bleeding. Val had cut her skin with his toenail.

"I am fine, thank you," she said as she regained her composure. Dolly moved forward again toward Val's right leg and grabbed ahold of his ankle. Meanwhile, Tim grabbed ahold of Val's left ankle and secured it with an ankle restraint tethered to the bed. Dolly then restrained Val's right ankle.

He bellowed, "Let me go! Let me go home and see my dog. I will come back in one hour and fifteen minutes."

Again, the nurses looked at me with another question on their faces, Why one hour and fifteen minutes?

I shrugged my shoulders. "Beats me," I said. I had no idea why Val had picked one hour and fifteen minutes. Why not just one hour? I never knew what he was thinking, seeing, or sensing as he journeyed down the mind's road of alcohol withdrawal.

Val kept demanding to be released. Then pleaded. Then demanded again. I stood behind the nurses and watched my husband—no longer the young, virile man I married. Addiction had robbed his looks, health, and desire to live. I glanced down at his restraints, then moved my eyes up to meet his eyes—cold and dark, like a deep, motionless pool of water along a wintry riverbank. Behind the steely eyes, I saw the beaten-down man: a man who craved alcohol, perhaps even loved alcohol as he had once loved me, and in turn, alcohol had repaid him by ripping the fabric of his life. Tears welled in my eyes, and I could not bear to watch him continue his rant.

"I am going to go home now," I told the nurses. "I can't watch him like this—restrained and ranting. I will be back in the morning."

I turned and left the room. As I walked to the car, I wondered how slowly the evening hours would pass for Val. Would he be agitated? Would he sleep?

Later that night, maybe 10:30, the phone rang. It was the night shift lead nurse, Tim. He said, "Val has been asking nonstop to talk with you. Will you talk with him and see if it will calm him?"

"Sure," I said and took in a deep breath.

I heard Tim talking to Val and telling him I was on the phone. Val said in a calm voice, "Hello, Kym?"

"Yes, it is me," I replied.

"Come and get me. I need to go home. I am all better."

"I can't take you home, Val. Your oxygen and heart need to be monitored, and you are going through alcohol withdrawal. You have to stay in the hospital tonight."

"Please," he pleaded. "Come get me."

"I can't."

His tone of malice erupted as he said, "You bitch! Who are you with?"

Tim took the phone from him and said, "I am so sorry. I believed him when he said he wanted to talk with you, and I gave him the benefit of my doubt."

I reassured Tim and said, "His behavior isn't surprising. He lashes out at me when I don't comply with his needs or expectations. It is all right, and please, call me anytime."

"I will," Tim replied. "He barely sleeps. He is agitated almost all the time."

"I know he is struggling. Thank you for telling me."

I hung up the phone. Shuffling back to bed, I rubbed my eyes and thought about the countless times he had called me names, trying to hurt me, degrade me. Like a mud pot, his anger was always percolating inside, occasionally spitting out a big blob of ugly mud toward me if I was not attending to his needs. His anger was deep-rooted and often uncontrollable. He had been resentful since he was a young child, bitter toward his parents and siblings, obsessively suspicious of their intentions.

I am reminded of a childhood story he shared many years ago. One afternoon after baseball practice, he walked into his home and smelled the intoxicating aroma of garlic, smoked bacon, and melted cheese on the pizzas his father had just brought home for the family dinner. Val, famished from baseball practice, tore into the box, grabbing a heavenly, hot slice of pizza. Just as he was ready to sink his teeth into the wonderful pie, he felt a heavy hand cup the back of his neck, slamming his head into the pizza box.

His father, keeping the force of his hand on the back of Val's neck, told him, "You disrespectful little bastard! How dare you take a piece of pizza before we all sit down at the dinner table."

Val attempted to explain that he was hungry, but his father would have none of his excuses. He was always telling Val to stop defending himself and do what he was told. Val was defeated, time and time again, by his father's physical and verbal abuse, diminishing his desire to communicate—until the mud pot erupted, spewing mucky, ugly words.

I witnessed his father's dark side—often in conflict with his son's—raising his voice and name-calling. And it didn't shadow just the four sons. He was condescending and unkind to his wife, calling her names if she was making too much noise in the kitchen or if dinner was late. And when she treated herself to a bowl of ice cream, he called her a fat pig.

I was always struck by his ability to be entertaining guests or having a holiday meal, and when he was done entertaining, although all the guests were still in his home, he would get up from his leather recliner, pass guests and family members, and walk down the hallway to his bedroom. Sometimes he wished all a good night, and sometimes he slipped away without a word, never returning to see guests off into the cold, dark evening or wishing them a safe drive home. Life was about him. I understood why Val disliked his father, and why he became his father.

CHAPTER 7—THE SPOON

As I drove home from the hospital, I thought about Val's mom and how much she loved her ice cream—so much that she didn't care that her husband called her a fat pig. Then my thoughts drifted to my ice cream spat with Val. It had begun one evening when we lived in Wyoming.

Soon after our move to Jackson, Wyoming, in 1999, Val's daily drinking moved from 5:00 p.m. to 3:00 p.m. By the time I was done working in my home office for the day, he was wrapped in his warm blanket of alcohol, his mood elevated in excitement and talkativeness. I, on the other hand, tired from working all day, wanted to sit, relax, and clear my mind for a few minutes—be in the present moment, not thinking about tomorrow's tasks or what I didn't accomplish today.

Val was pleasant for the first hour, telling me about the day's news and little projects he had worked on. After all, he had not been employed for the past five years, other than some small consulting projects I could assign to him. I did my best to pay attention because he often complained that I did not pay attention to him during the day. He didn't understand why I could not take a midafternoon break to visit with him, maybe even have sex with him (yes, I heard that often). After his first hour of talkativeness, his mood would shift from upbeat to impatient, happy to irritable, and attentive to inattentive. Our conversations turned to monologues, as he dismissed my thoughts. Not having the same point of view sent him back to his childhood, where being misunderstood or denied a voice created frustration and anger. The unheard child often reared its ugly head, giving Val his voice—the hurtful voice.

One evening, after cleaning up after dinner and putting the last pot in the cupboard, Val pulled the vanilla ice cream from the freezer—his second favorite dessert, after his mom's homemade chocolate cake. He put heaping spoonfuls of vanilla ice cream into a large bowl, adding a generous pour of Hershey's Chocolate Syrup on top and stirring it all together in the bowl until it resembled a milkshake. When he started, he stirred in slow, methodical circles, but then, becoming impatient, he powered through the hard ice cream, slightly bending the serving spoon. Instead of retrieving the ice cream scoop, he made a second attempt to stir with the serving spoon, bending the handle almost ninety degrees.

"Val, why don't you use the ice cream scoop?" I snapped. "That is the second spoon you have ruined!"

"This spoon is fine. Why do you care about a stupid spoon?" he barked.

"Because it is part of a silverware set, and you are ruining the silverware. Why can't you use the ice scream scoop?" I asked, again.

He looked chastened, then his face hardened.

"You are a bitch! Here, you freak," he said, throwing the spoon in the sink and stomping out of the kitchen.

The next day, we discussed the spoon. "I am sorry," he said sheepishly. "I should have used the ice cream scoop."

"It is not about the spoon," I replied. "It is all the seemingly little arguments we have over the smallest of situations that cause tension between us or, worse, name-calling and yelling." I paused, then continued, "We do not have these arguments during the day. I believe alcohol causes the drama in the evenings."

"I disagree it is the drinking. I do not get sloppy drunk or pass out at night. I can manage my drinking."

"Would you please have your first drink later, maybe after dinner?"

"Yes, I will have my first drink a little later in the evening and drink less."

I nodded in agreement and smiled, knowing the pattern would repeat. A continual cycle: wash, rinse, repeat. Each time I tried to discuss alcohol, he would deny having a problem, assuring me he was just a social drinker. He would ask, "Do I fall down drunk? Do I black out? Do I not get up the next morning?" He never used the word "alcoholic." Never.

I knew but didn't accept that I was powerless over his drinking. And I would continue, for years turning into decades, to focus on the alcoholic: trying to help him, trying to fix him, trying to fix his disease. Yet, for decades, I doubted alcohol was a disease. My parents were alcoholics; they started abusing alcohol to self-medicate and escape challenges in their midlives—unable to hold jobs and enjoy a lifestyle they had relished in their younger years. My father's incarceration strongly affected the rest of their lives. The same was true for Val. His formative years, being raised by an alcoholic father, affected the rest of his life. My parents and Val embraced alcohol to ease their emotional pains, instead of dealing with their emotions. Perhaps for some, the beginning stages of drinking is a choice to ease unresolved emotional issues, but later the brain and body require the daily alcohol to function, creating an addiction: a disease. As the disease progresses, and there are negative physical and mental effects, the awareness of choice becomes more difficult, and the willingness to get treatment even harder. But my experience was that choice always remained part of the process, for both the alcoholic and the family member of the alcoholic.

Eventually, I would stop focusing on the alcoholic and start focusing on myself—managing what I could manage—my own life. But that was many years away, and I still had the bent spoon in my silverware drawer.

After the spoon spat, I decided that since Val dismissed my concerns about his drinking, then perhaps he would listen to a professional. We could learn how to communicate and stop arguing over little things. We communicated about the big things—home purchases, financial goals, and retirement dreams—but good grief, we couldn't agree on what spoon to use to scoop ice cream!

Why?

To my surprise, a week following the spoon incident, he agreed to see a marriage counselor. I had an agenda, trying to fix the alcoholic, and I was hopeful a professional could guide Val to understand that he was an alcoholic or at least address his drinking and its impact on our partnership. It never occurred to me that he too had an agenda—which I learned after our meeting with the marriage counselor.

To the reader, are you counting how many Do Nots of being in an alcoholic family I have broken? Do Not create a crisis (arguing over a spoon), Do Not push anyone but yourself (monitoring alcohol intake and suggesting the alcoholic drink less), and Do Not manipulate situations (suggesting we go to a marriage counselor to address alcoholism instead of discussing our marriage). If I were in grade school and wrote "Going forward, I will not" on the chalkboard 100 times, I would have more than 100 stories to finish each sentence.

I had a pattern of disingenuous communication. I didn't know how to communicate with an alcoholic. In a relationship with an alcoholic, I learned to suppress my thoughts to cope or survive. But this suppression, or Tolerance, is unhealthy. I needed to learn to "say what I mean and mean what I say."

Our meeting with the counselor, Marilynn, was with both of us at first, then with an individual follow-up. During the first meeting, we shared our stories about evening spats, including the bent spoon. We discussed alcohol, and I shared that I believed it was affecting our relationship. She provided simple tools on how to communicate and sent us on our way. A week later, she met with us individually, first with Val, and then with me. When I sat down to discuss my relationship with Val, I was excited that I could reveal how often Val drank and how his behavior was sometimes abusive. I needed to vent and I needed confirmation. But to my surprise, she started the conversation by telling me how alcohol affects relationships, and how it is difficult to have a "normal" partnership when alcohol clouds judgment and heightens emotions. She explained how it affects our ability to perceive reality, and we distort reality through our impaired lens.

Yes, you are exactly right, I thought.

I started to respond, and she continued her thought, saying, "That is why you have to stop drinking so much wine."

I was shocked! Speechless! I thought, *I am the one who must stop drinking? We are seeing you because I want you—no, I need you—to tell Val he drinks too much and can't control his emotions. Unbelievable! How did Val persuade the marriage counselor that I was the one with a drinking problem—a disease?*

He had had an agenda: deny his excessive drinking, project it onto me, deflect and blame, and hide the truth. He had relieved himself from any personal responsibility and made me the bad actor.

I didn't know what to say to Marilynn. I explained that Val was the alcoholic, not me. She repeated that alcohol, regardless of who is drinking, can cause dysfunction in a relationship.

Defeated, I left the meeting knowing Val blamed me, like the time he got his DUI. He was the master manipulator, the blame shifter. I too played my part by not seeing how I had made mistakes in living with an alcoholic. I had marched down the PATH of monitoring his alcohol consumption and then losing objectivity and getting Angry—arguing with the alcoholic. When I was exhausted from those tactics, I had tried manipulating Val by using a marriage counselor to do my bidding. I wanted her to fix him so he would stop drinking and behave as I saw fit. I imagine most couples seeking a marriage counselor are seeking a judge—someone to rule who is right and who is wrong. Power is the domain of control. How do you have control? By having the other person believe you are right, not wrong. If Val proved I had a drinking problem and couldn't control myself, then he was right: he was not an alcoholic, and he had the power, and he did not need the comfort of surrendering to the evening siren.

We both struggled to be right or to appear right. And what happened? We argued, again and again. A good counselor would have helped us defuse the power struggle and understand the issues, giving us tools to work through them. Providing tools to communicate in a principled way, not a power-based way.

I drove away from the counselor's office feeling defeated. Alone, feeling unable to share my problems and concerns with Val, a professional counselor, or family. On my journey with an alcoholic, I was on my PATH, straddling Anger and Tolerance. I made the mistake of allowing my aloneness to prevent me from finding another counselor or confidante—that mistake would soon propel me into Tolerance. But I was still angry and wanted to scream!

And I did scream!

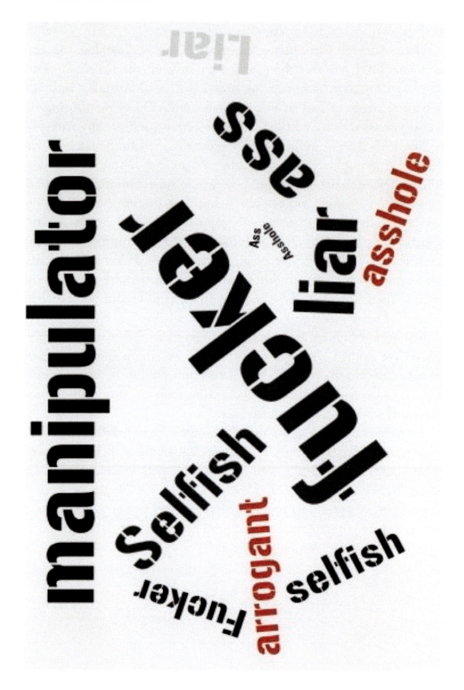

Chapter 8—She Sells Seashells

DAY 3. I woke up early that morning, suddenly remembering that the garbage truck would be rumbling down the street by 7:00. Remembering yesterday's conversation with the intensivist, him bluntly telling me to clean the house of all the alcohol, emphasizing that Val could never drink or smoke again—his body would not survive it—I hurried and collected the bottles. Spinning the lazy Susan in the kitchen, I stopped it halfway, reaching in to remove everything with alcohol on the ingredients list: half-gallon containers of whiskey, wine bottles, gin, marsala, dry sherry, and vermouth. *There is no reason to keep anything that will remind Val of alcohol*, I thought as I removed the margarita salt, simple syrup, and lime juice.

I set all the bottles upon the kitchen counter, opened them, and methodically emptied each one down the drain, gagging at the smell of red wine, thinking how awful it smells in the morning and how pleasant it smells in the evening—swirling a glass and smelling the aroma.

All done! I placed the empty bottles in the recycle can. Next mission: locate all cigarette and marijuana paraphernalia.

Back in the master bathroom, I opened the sink cupboard and retrieved a small wooden box, its once shiny finish now dull and tacky from marijuana-resin-coated fingertips opening and closing the lid, day after day, year after year. Val has kept this box for thirty years. I opened it and removed the contents: a glass pipe, rolling papers, lighters, an ounce of marijuana, and a small plastic bong. In the corner lay a three-inch, silver, molded hand making a peace sign. I stopped for a moment and felt the little statue in my hand—rubbing my fingers back and forth across the cold metal. I thought about the story

69

behind the peace statue. Val, as a young boy, didn't spend much time with his father—they rarely played ball together, set up Hot Wheels racetracks, or built models. His father wasn't interested in such foolish, time-wasting projects, and he certainly wasn't interested in spending quality bonding time with his son. Val would hang out with Keith, the next-door neighbor, a young man in his twenties who befriended Val and helped him with his guy projects, such as building a go-cart and a tree fort. Val looked up to Keith and they spent a lot of time together—Keith was a father figure, and Val cherished his time with him. Val was in junior high when Keith died in a motorcycle accident, and Val felt the pain of losing a good friend. Keith had given the peace statue to Val before his untimely death, and Val kept it as a reminder of the father figure and confidant he had lost too soon in his formative years.

I rolled the little statue back and forth in the palm of my hand and then decided I would keep it—find a new keepsake place. I set the statue down and concentrated on the tasks ahead. I tossed the remaining box items into the wastebasket. Then I took the wastebasket to the next room to get more paraphernalia from the living room's television hutch. Hidden behind a tall oval ceramic vase was another bong and a small baggie of marijuana. I scooped them up and added them to the wastebasket. I could hear the disposal truck coming down the street. *Just one more stop*, I thought, and headed to the garage. I found another half gallon of Canadian Club in Val's tool cabinet. I had successfully purged the house of everything related to alcohol, tobacco, and marijuana.

Leaving the recycle and garbage cans behind me as I slowly walked back up the driveway, I was in no hurry to shower and get ready for another visit to the hospital. Yesterday, the nurses had told me that Val probably would not remember my being there, but I wanted to be there in case they were wrong. I was hopeful that somewhere deep in his mind he would know I was there, talking to him and being supportive while he was in the ICU. I felt empathy for him, and yet I no longer loved him. He had to start caring about himself and stop drinking, and I knew I had to move along my PATH to Healing.

Two hours later, I drove into the hospital parking lot. I took my usual route to the ICU, stopped at the coffee stand for a latte, then rode the elevator to the third floor. I pressed the big red button to notify the

ICU staff I was at the entrance, then stepped back and waited for the Queen's Guard to swing toward me. I walked through the doorway and turned left to walk directly ahead to Val's room—a corner room barely visible by the nursing staff and difficult to keep a watch on.

The bedding was new and neatly made. The inside curtains were drawn back. The counters were bare, with no sign of cups, toothpaste, or a toothbrush. The room was empty. For a second my heart raced, and I thought, *Oh my God, Val died!* I kept walking toward the room until I came to the corner counter of the nursing workstation. I saw Paul, and he walked toward me.

"Good morning," he said with a smile. He was the jokester in the ICU and always had a smile on his face and something witty to say. "He has been a bad boy," he said with a crooked grin. "We moved Val to room 442 so we could keep a better eye on him; he has been a troublemaker, and he was very agitated last night."

Paul gestured me toward room 442. We walked together, and Paul slid the curtain panel to the side and motioned with an open palm for me to enter. A young man was talking to Val. Paul introduced me to Chris and said he was a nurse's aide who visited alcoholic patients to help redirect their focus and turn their attention away from the detox process. Karen, another nurse, was also in the room, hanging more bags on the IV stand.

Paul pointed out that Karen had shaved Val that morning. Karen turned to me, her face tense, and rigidly said, "And I will never shave him again. He accused me of trying to kill him. I nearly nicked him with the razor when he jerked away from me and yelled for help."

As Karen told me about shaving Val, I thought, *I wonder what else he said to her to make her so tense and stern. I bet he was a jerk and said something sexual or nasty. Yep, he is going to be like the nun—a revolting, foul-mouthed patient.*

Karen finished her story and turned back to the monitors. Chris had been leaning on the left side bar of Val's bed, and he stood up and shook my hand. "Nice to meet you, Kym," he said. "Your husband and I have been having a chat this morning. It seems he wants to leave the hospital, and I have been explaining why he can't leave."

Chris had to have been about thirty years old, though he looked barely old enough to legally drink. I presumed he was older because he had graduated from college, had worked a few years at hospitals, and was applying to be a police officer. His bedside manner was indicative of a police officer, not a nurse's aide or a caseworker. When he spoke, he was calm but blunt. He reminded me of all the times I had tried to speak rationally with Val about alcohol consumption, thinking he would understand me and agree with my point of view. Chris was going to distract Val at best, but most likely only irritate him. As I had previously learned, the staff reiterated the facts, knowing that there were times the patient would be irrational or delusional. Chris's interaction with Val would cause one of those instances.

I pulled my phone from my purse as Chris started talking with Val again. Before I had arrived, Val had been telling Chris he wanted to go home, and Chris had been explaining, again, why Val could not go home.

I turned on the phone's video recorder and pointed the camera toward Chris and Val. I held the phone down low, below my belt buckle, hoping not to be noticed. Val would throw a temper tantrum if he knew I was videoing him. I wanted a video of Val during his detox. I planned to share the video with him after he was released from the hospital to remind him of the effects of alcohol withdrawal and hopefully spur him to join a recovery program. I had been asking him for years to consider joining AA or any support group. The video would help with my plea for him to get help.

To the reader, are you still counting how many Do Nots of being in an alcoholic family I continued to break? Even in the ICU, I continued to practice the Do Not disallow the alcoholic to experience the consequences of their own actions. The ICU was the ultimate consequence of Val's drinking, and I was still trying to guide him to recovery.

I looked down at my phone to make sure it was recording, then looked up at Val. I will never forget the image of him at that moment. An image that can still bring me to tears. He was wearing a yellow-and-white hospital gown; it was twisted around his stomach, which was still grossly distended. A blanket was pulled up over his legs. Soft blue Velcro pads were wrapped around his wrists, cushioning the white cotton straps with plastic snap-in buckles that tethered his wrists to the bed rails. His left hand had splashes of purple and blue from hitting it against the bed rails.

Looking at his chest and face, I saw that the IV had been moved to his chest because he had incessantly picked at the needle in his hand. A white plastic oxygen mask was strapped around the back of his ears, and the mask was cockeyed under his nose—looking like a large white mustache. Eyes shut tight, he was squeezing his eyebrows, making creases in his forehead. His lower lip jutted out, and the corners of his mouth were turned down, pressing into new cold sores. The light behind him was shining on top of his head, making his dark brown hair appear golden and silky soft. His face was blotchy and his cheeks puffy, ready to catch the tears as they slowly rolled down. He looked as though he was contemplating, *I am so miserable. I have no joy left. Please God, I just want to die.* I felt empathy, sadness, and, oddly, calmness. I was thinking about how I was going to take care of myself. Do what was best for me—that was coming soon.

Then his eyes popped open. He had a look of determination like a trial lawyer ready to recite his opening statement. He said to Chris, "I want to go home. I am better. Look at the monitors; all my readings are good."

Chris responded, "What you need to do is just admit that you have to wait. I know you want to take an active role because you are a go-get-it kind of guy, but right now you must take a back seat and let us help you. Let us help you help yourself."

Val turned his head away from Chris. I could tell he wasn't going to agree with Chris. No, he was thinking of something factual, powerful, for his case.

Chris continued, "You need to listen to us."

Val's lips pinched tight together and he started to look angry. He continued to look away from Chris, clutching the white blanket with both his hands.

Chris continued, "Hopefully, you have never been in a hospital before. I know this is probably scary to you, but we do this every day. We make our living helping people."

As Chris spoke, Val took a deep breath and parted his lips. He was ready to combat Chris.

Val released the blanket and turned his head slightly toward Chris. "I am not going to drop dead in one hour and ten minutes," he said in a shaky voice as he raised his left hand to take ahold of the bed rail.

"If we don't fix these problems, you might die," Chris responded.

"I might."

"You can't drive when you are on these medications. You would probably run into something."

"I don't feel delirious. My vision is not slurred."

Chris stopped Val and said, "All right. Listen to yourself. You just used the word 'slurred' to explain your vision. 'Slurred' is used for speech. And, by the way, your speech is slurred!"

To this, Val said nothing.

Chris then told Val to say "She sells seashells by the seashore."

"She . . ." Val paused. He looked up at Chris, his eyes asking him to repeat the request.

Chris obliged and repeated the old tongue twister: "She sells seashells by the seashore."

Staring hard at Chris, Val said, "She shells seasells by the sheshore."

"All right, do you hear yourself?"

"Yes."

Chris started to say, "Now . . ."

But Val interrupted with a grunt, pointing his right finger up at Chris. He cleared his throat and continued, "My first optha, my first ophthalmologist said forty-five minutes. I am going to ask you three questions. He said remember pencil, watch, and forklift."

"Pencil, watch, and what?" I asked, remembering the three words the neurologist, not ophthalmologist, from Mayo Clinic had given Val during his neuropathy testing: pencil, watch, and chair. I was surprised that Val had remembered two of the three objects.

Val responded confidently, "And a forklift. Remember?" He licked his lips and continued, "He put me through it, and at the end, he said, 'What were the three words?' And I said, 'Pencil, watch, and forklift.'"

Val was trying to demonstrate that he had his mental faculties and could think clearly. He was determined to convince Chris he could go home.

Chris said, "That was a good idea. How about we do the same thing again?"

I asked, "Do you want to do three new words?"

Our distraction was not going to last much longer. Val was trying to demonstrate that he was reasoning clearly, and Chris and I ignored him and tried to continue with the verbal game. I knew all too well that when someone did not give Val the response he desired, he became defensive.

Sure enough, Val turned his head toward me and scowled. He stared, not blinking for several seconds. He looked disgusted with me.

Chris observed Val staring at me and said, "Do you remember what you just told us was a good idea?"

Val parted his lips as though ready to say something. His chest moved up as he took a deep breath. He continued to stare.

I said, "Are you staring at me? Chris is talking to you."

Several more seconds passed, and Chris waved his hand in front of Val's face. Val blinked his eyes rapidly and stopped staring. He looked at me and said, "You know how I feel about doctors. I have been against doctors all my life."

"Yes, I know," I said with a half-hearted laugh.

He placed his left hand on the bed rail, then slightly raised his right hand and pointed his index finger at me. He said with disapproval, "And the fact that I keep letting you watch." He paused. "Watch people pin me down."

He stopped talking and stared into my eyes.

Chris smirked.

Still pointing his finger, Val nonsensically said, "And you keep talking my social ring to your social ring."

Another pause. He blankly stared at me. "I don't talk around your medical ring about you."

I politely responded, "Val, no one is pinning you down. The staff restrained you to keep you safe, but no one is forcefully pinning you down. Why would you think such a thing?"

He struggled to pull himself upright in the bed while staring at me with disdain. I had seen the look many times before. Anytime he did not get his way, he gave me that "I hate you" look. It was easier to blame me for his woes than to take responsibility for his actions. In our earlier years, he had blamed his parents for his failures and low self-esteem, but since his parents died, I had been the target of his anger.

Val informed us, "I am going home for fifteen minutes, and then I am coming back. And nothing is stopping me."

Chris responded, "I have news for you. Nothing is going to stop me from keeping you here. I am in opposition of your idea to leave. Sadly, you cannot win this battle. We cannot let you leave the hospital for any reason until all the doctors that are assigned to your case have cleared you. All right?"

Val started rocking his right leg back and forth like a petulant child. He continued for a few moments, then tried to raise both of his arms up and asked, "Well, what am I doing here?"

"You are getting medication," Chris said.

"And I have had my medication," Val replied.

"Do you want to go through a list of the symptoms you still have?"

"No, I hear my symptoms every day. No, I don't need to hear them again."

I interjected, "That is why you are here. Your symptoms aren't better. The doctors are trying to get your heart healthy and . . ."

Val cut me off with a raised voice: "So talking about it is going to make it better?"

I said, "You just asked why you are here."

Seeing Val's irritation, Chris said, "We are giving you medications."

Val placed his hands next to his hips and huffed. "All the medications are already in me."

Chris said, "No, we are giving them to you slowly." He pointed to the IV stand and the bags hanging from it. He said, "We can't give them to you all at once. We must make it a slow drip. That is why it is taking so long."

Val stopped talking. He knew he was not going to get his way and leave the hospital. Pouting, he stared at the wall ahead of him.

Chris continued, "The best thing you can do is try to get some sleep. When you wake up, we can talk about this a little bit more levelheadedly."

Val did not respond. Pursing his lips tight until they turned whitish, he stared at his feet; he'd lost the battle and decided to ignore us. A moment later he turned his attention to the wrist restraints. He lifted his right hand over toward his left and tried to reach the plastic snap buckle. He could not reach it. Defeated, he closed his eyes and pretended to sleep.

Chris had suggested to Val that when he woke up and was levelheaded, we could talk about his hospital stay. I feared that levelheadedness was not going to occur. Val had been in denial for years and did not take responsibility for his actions. Why would he be levelheaded during detox? I knew tomorrow was going to bring more of the same behavior. Detox can take up to a week, and it was just day three.

CHAPTER 9—MAN'S BEST FRIEND

DAY 4. The phone rang early that morning. It was the hospital nurse assigned to Val's room for the day shift. It was the same nurse who had been assigned to Val yesterday, and she was familiar with his case.

"Val had a bad night," she said. "He was agitated all evening and barely slept."

"It has been four days. I thought the first three days were the worst for acute withdrawal. Shouldn't he be improving?"

She hesitated and replied in a concerned tone, "Depending on how long he has been drinking and how much he has been drinking, his withdrawal could last longer."

"Are his hallucinations better?"

"No."

"What can be done to help him?"

"We are having trouble balancing his medications to reduce the effects of alcohol withdrawal and his severe agitation. We are also going to take some liver tests."

"All right. Should I come in later this afternoon to learn about the liver test results?"

"No, the results will not be complete. We will continue to monitor him and try to get him to rest. He isn't sleeping but more than ten minutes at a time. Right now, your presence agitates him. He wants to go home, and when he realizes he can't go home, he gets angry. Stay home today and let him rest."

"All right. Is there anything else I can do?"

"When you visit tomorrow, bring a few personal items, a favorite blanket or perhaps some family pictures. Personal items help patients feel more at home and result in helping them to relax and stay calm."

"I am sure you would really appreciate any help in keeping him calm. He is not exactly a model patient!"

"No, not exactly, but we have had worse."

I laughed and thanked her as I hung up the phone. *Surprising,* I thought, *the hospital waited until now to run certain liver tests. I am sure the years of heavy drinking have taken their toll on Val's organs. He is fortunate to be in the ICU.*

I sank into the couch and sighed with exhaustion. Three days visiting Val in the ICU had been incredibly stressful, having to witness the dark ghouls of withdrawal torture his mind and body.

I got up off the couch and walked back into the bedroom. I lifted my dog onto the bed, and together, we closed our eyes and went back to sleep for three hours. It was a deep sleep and I felt rested when I woke. As I lay in bed, I thought, *Tomorrow is another day, and hopefully Val will be better. But what if he isn't better? What will the doctors and nurses do to help him?*

Rubbing my eyes, I stretched, made my way out of bed, and took a long hot shower. After dressing, I remembered my morning conversation and the request to take a few personal items to the hospital. I went to the curio cabinet and looked at the framed pictures from some of our favorite moments: Old Faithful in Yellowstone National Park, the two of us with our motorcycles standing in front of an old lookout tower, a moose standing on our back deck in snowy Jackson, and the four dogs we had adopted and loved. I took a few dog pictures from the cabinet. My favorite was a picture of BJ, a golden retriever we raised as a puppy for Canine Companions for Independence, sitting in front of a Christmas tree on the first day we adopted him.

I was certain Val would like these pictures, especially of BJ. Val had taken BJ to his training class every Saturday and had helped with his daily training exercises: sit, stay, leave it, back up, here. The following day, we would take BJ on a field trip, going into restaurants and grocery stores, practicing walking around strangers. We had so much fun showing off his commands and telling elated baby-talking puppy admirers about the Canine Companions for Independence program. We reveled in puppy raising and shared sadness and tears when surrendering him to the Santa Rosa Training Center for his new life as a support companion.

I smiled as I held each picture frame, tracing the outline of the dog's face, reminding me of the loving and delightful memories with each dog: camping, hiking, and outdoor adventures. I was overwhelmed with a sense of joy, an unexpected visitor at my guesthouse. I had not felt joy for so long. My smile widened with the memory of the earlier years, my husband, so kind and compassionate, not just toward his own dogs, but to all companion animals. We had volunteered with fundraisers, walked our dogs in walkathons, golfed in charity events, and later, after relocating to Jackson, had volunteered with the local animal shelter and PAWS of Jackson Hole. In the early years, before he needed a drink at 3:00 p.m., he was kind and extroverted with the other volunteers—passionate and giving. We enjoyed life together as well as shared experiences with others. We were partners on our path of a shared life.

His passion for life faded as the years of drinking robbed him of his desire to give anything of himself. He was consumed with self-pity and negative thoughts. Alcohol had ravaged his heart, his very need to connect to others, and had left him feeling empty and alone.

After his visits to Mayo Clinic, he seemed void of any hope of physical improvement. A few months before he was admitted to the ICU, he had a loose tooth and would play with it—wiggling it between his fingers and pushing his tongue against the back of the tooth. I suggested he go to the dentist, and he scoffed at the idea, asking me, "Why would I want to go to the dentist when they are just going to pull it? I can pull it." A few minutes later, he walked into the bathroom with a pair of pliers, clamped his tooth with the pliers, and yanked downward—out popped the tooth! He held up the tooth, stared for a moment, and said, "Why does it matter if I pull my own tooth? I am going to die anyway. I feel it."

He set the pliers down, picked up the tooth, and walked away. I stared at the back of his head as he turned the corner and disappeared down the hallway. He seemed indifferent to life, giving up and waiting to die.

CHAPTER 10—THE HUG LADY

DAY 5. Placing the framed dog pictures into my oversized purse, I collected my sweater, coffee mug, and keys and set out for the hospital.

I pulled into the hospital parking lot and saw that the space under the tree was vacant. I parked and walked into the main lobby, giving a cheerful "good morning" to the volunteers at the front desk. I turned left and headed down the hallway to the elevators. As I pushed the elevator button, a tall Scandinavian lady with shiny silver-gray hair walked up and stood beside me. It was Val's cardiologist.

We rode up the elevator together and exchanged pleasantries. As she used her badge to open the Queen's Guard to the ICU, she turned to me and said, "I will see you and your husband in a few minutes."

"Thank you. I look forward to an update," I replied.

I walked to room 442 and pulled the curtains to the side to find Val lying in bed, sound asleep—his face relaxed, washed with peace. I sat down in the big chair beside his bed, lifted his tethered left hand, and cupped my hands around it, gently holding his hand and whispering to him that I was there.

A half hour passed, and the cardiologist entered his room. "Good morning, again," she said with a pleasant smile. I liked her. She was grandmotherly—kind and pleasant—and her accent was charming.

"Good morning," I replied, standing up from the big chair.

"We ran several tests yesterday. Val's liver is extended and swollen. There is no bleeding in the brain."

I was surprised that the doctors had looked for bleeding in the brain. No one mentioned being concerned about his brain. I said nothing and waited for more details.

"He has been sedated. We have not been able to find a way to keep your husband from being over-sedated and yet be safe to himself and others. Last night he had a fit, and he kicked another nurse during his physical and emotional outburst."

"He kicked *another* nurse? This is the second time."

"Yes. He kicked Karen. He was able to swing his leg up for a blow to her side. Thankfully, she is all right."

"Thank goodness. Is this still alcohol detox causing his erratic behavior?"

"Yes. We are changing medications to a Valium and antipsychotic mix. We are trying to find the right mix that will let Val come out of the withdrawal and be safe."

"I never knew detox was so hard on the mind. I always thought the body just had sweats and shakes."

"Unfortunately, no. Alcohol withdrawal can be harder on the brain than the alcohol itself. And he may have permanent neurological damage."

My heart felt heavy. I was worried. I thought, *What if he has neurological damage? What are we going to do—how is he going to live with the pain from his neuropathy and other neurological issues? What could those issues be? How am I going to take care of him? I no longer want to be responsible!*

The cardiologist then discussed Val's heart for a few more minutes. Changing the subject, she said, "The pulmonologist will be in to check on Val today. Val is not swallowing his saliva, and it is draining down his throat and into his lungs. The pulmonologist might put Val on a ventilator. The ventilator will help him breathe and keep fluids from building up in his lungs."

"He would not want to be on a ventilator," I replied.

"He may not have a choice. He could get pneumonia and die," she said. She tried not to show emotion, but it was obvious that she was worried.

The cardiologist left the room to continue her rounds. I sat back down in the chair. I sat there and watched Val breathe. He looked peaceful, and I wondered what war was being fought inside his body. What would he be feeling if he weren't sedated and taking a cocktail of drugs? I felt sad for him. He had really messed up his life—his precious life.

I took the pictures from my purse and placed them on the side table. I hoped Val would notice them when he awakened. I stood up and pushed the big chair back under the window. I collected my purse, phone, and sweater. I bent over the bed and kissed Val on the forehead, told him to rest, and said goodbye. As I was leaving the room, the social worker, Judy, was walking toward me. We had briefly met the night Val was checked into the ICU.

"How are you doing, honey?" she asked with genuine compassion.

"I am all right—a little overwhelmed," I replied.

She looked at the pictures. "Beautiful dogs. He will appreciate having them here. Do you want to talk for a while? I have a wide shoulder you can lean on."

"Sure, I think it would be good for me. I feel like I have bottled up so many years of my life."

"Let's go down to the cafeteria and have a cup of coffee—my treat."

"I would like that," I said, and she put her arm around me as we walked together to the cafeteria.

We started with pleasant conversation. I asked her how she had gotten involved in the health care field and how often she volunteered. She asked me how I had decided to live in Tucson. Then I told her I was thinking about attending Al-Anon, that I needed to share as well as listen to others who might have had similar experiences with an alcoholic. She smiled and said, "I think that is a fabulous idea; you will find other people's experiences and stories insightful, and they might help you in your life with an alcoholic."

"But I want to understand the alcoholic," I professed.

She shifted in her chair and started to explain. "Al-Anon follows the Twelve Steps originally crafted by AA. The Steps apply to the family members too, just a bit differently since you do not have substance abuse. As you know, substance abuse changes people in permanent ways—it can permanently alter their personality. But like the alcoholic, your behavior changes with each stage of alcoholism as you navigate the turbulent waters of the alcoholic's irrational thinking. You will learn a lot about yourself as you listen to the stories of others in Al-Anon."

"I won't learn about the alcoholic?" I asked.

"No . . . Well, yes, but indirectly through community sharing and literature. Al-Anon does not teach about the alcoholic; in fact, attendees are encouraged not to focus on the alcoholic but to focus on their own actions and how they interact and respond to the alcoholic's behavior. It helps you to see how your desire to rationalize with an irrational addict will often lead to your own irrational behavior."

I shared stories about my behavior with Judy. I explained that I had tried changing him, helping him, finding projects and work for him, covering for him, and spending less time with family because of him, and I had lost my objectivity. I had argued, yelled, cried, said nothing, and suppressed my own thoughts and interests. I had even drunk with him, numbing my mind to tolerate his behavior. I agreed with Judy: it would be helpful to hear how others have lived with an alcoholic and the choices they have made to cope.

I took a sip of my coffee and said, "But I really want to understand Val. Why would he do this to himself? It doesn't make any sense that he would let his body deteriorate."

Judy interjected, "Kym, you continue to think logically and rationally about an irrational addict. The clinical stages of alcoholism are defined in the Jellinek Curve. There are behavioral changes with each stage (figure 3). For example, in the early stage, the alcoholic may have an urgency for a first drink or may hide drinks; in the middle stage, the alcoholic may become irritable and argumentative and may have work and money troubles; and in the late stage, the alcoholic has impaired thinking, paranoia, health problems, and a poorer quality of life."

Judy noticed I was taking notes and stopped a moment to let me write and ponder the new information I was absorbing.

"I carry a book that I often quote and recommend to family members who have an alcoholic loved one in the ICU. It is not uncommon for people admitted to the ICU with medical issues unrelated to alcohol to experience detox. The book might give you the answers you are looking for in finding clarity and understanding of the alcoholic." Judy pulled the book from her bag and showed it to me: *The Addictive Personality: Understanding the Addictive Process and Compulsive Behavior* by Craig Nakken. She opened the book to part 1 and read, "Addiction must be viewed as a process that is progressive."[6] She looked up at me and continued, "He explains that the person uses an object, such as a bottle of alcohol, to achieve a mood change, attempting to control or

6 . Nakken, *The Addictive Personality*, 1.

achieve a desired feeling—maybe hiding pain, sadness, or even giving one a sense of happiness."

"But I have enjoyed alcohol, and it can make me feel good—but I am not an alcoholic," I interjected before taking another sip of coffee.

Judy smiled. "But you are not using alcohol to bathe yourself in seductive mood changes. According to the author, for the prospective addict, the mood change is intense and starts off enjoyably, allowing the person to mistake the mood change for social comfort, self-esteem, or perhaps self-security. People turn toward addictive behavior when they don't like the way they are feeling."

I said, "But Val would openly express anger, even rage, he harbored for his father and brother Greg, and I know those are deep—bottom of the ocean deep—emotional scars. His deep anger was the result of years of verbal abuse and lack of intimacy and guidance from his father—an emotionally ill-equipped man who suffered his own abuses and addiction. His father trampled on Val's self-esteem and self-confidence, always telling Val he could never accomplish his goals or dreams. He once smashed Val's face into a pizza box because Val didn't behave the way his father expected him to."

She reached her hand out and touched mine. "You are right about Val's emotional scars. And he didn't like the way he was feeling."

She continued, "In natural relationships, people connect with friends and family, a spiritual higher power, self, or community to have healthy interdependencies. Those connections give us intimacy, guidance, growth, and a sense of being needed—not unlike the two of us talking now, sharing experiences, and connecting. As Craig Nakken explains in the 'Natural Relationships' section, an addictive personality doesn't connect with others; instead, they connect with an object (the alcohol bottle) and that takes the place of other people. They trade natural relationships with addictive relationships. Val turned to a bottle—and then turned inward, an emotional isolation."

I thought for a moment and said, "But Val wasn't always this way. He was my best friend and companion; we were so active together."

"I know, honey. When he was younger, he was himself. As he grew older and the addictive process progressed, another personality emerged. As Craig Nakken refers to this occurrence in 'Stage One: Internal Change,' he explains, 'The most important aspect of Stage One is the creation of this addictive personality: the Self and the Addict. The Self represents the "normal," human side of the addicted person, while the Addict represents the side that is consumed and transformed by the addiction.'[7] (Val struggled with the Self and the Addict.) Eventually, there is a loss of Self and the addictive personality is firmly in control, guiding the person to use addictive logic." Judy paused and selected the dog-eared page with the chapter title "Emotional Logic" and read, "'Addiction is very logical and follows a logical progression, but this progression is totally based on what I call *emotional logic*, not intellectual logic.'[8] Does that make sense to you?"

I nodded. "His addiction to alcohol was a slow process—maybe a decade of what I thought of as social drinking. I remember he started drinking daily when we lived on Whidbey Island, then he got a DUI. He was so ashamed and embarrassed—he dreaded telling me. But then he also embellished the story and blamed the event on the police who pulled him over and arrested him. Is that addictive logic? His story was not based on truth, and the problem was the police, not his own actions."

"I think you are correct."

We sat for a few minutes and cradled our warm coffee cups, taking an occasional sip. She continued, "I mentioned the four stages of alcoholism. It seems your husband may have been at the end of stage one, the early stage. In *The Addictive Personality*, the author refers to this phase as 'Stage One: Internal Change.' The next phase is the middle stage, which the author refers to as 'Stage Two: Lifestyle Change.' In this stage, the author explains that the addict will display behavioral issues where the person becomes more out of control, depending less on themselves and the people they love, and more on the addictive lifestyle and addictive logic. The Self personality slowly loses to the Addict personality. The Addict is often self-righteous and self-centered." Judy paused as she thumbed through the book to the section on Stage Two. She read, "To the addict, other people's concern is seen as a problem. People are seen as nosy, and their concern becomes an obstacle to be overcome. People—including the Self part of the personality—are unimportant unless they can be used to deepen the addiction. If not,

---

7. Nakken, *The Addictive Personality*, 25.
8. Nakken, *The Addictive Personality*, 8.

they are discarded."[9]

"Wow," I said, tapping the side of my coffee cup. "After all these years, that is exactly how I feel: used and depleted. All this time I was trying to help Val feel secure, be self-confident, and find purpose in life. In the beginning of our marriage, I thought he had optimism and the confidence to create and enjoy a good partnership together, but that all crumbled and fell away to him turning to alcohol for relief. I was just an annoyance when I didn't behave the way his addictive logic wanted me to behave."

I paused. "Let me share a story with you that exemplifies your description of the lifestyle change. Before I start, let me state that we had occasional disagreements because Val was acting out emotionally and I was always trying to respond rationally. It was the clash of emotional logic, or illogic, and rational logic—as I have now learned—the addictive logic and the rational logic. For example, we once fought over his having bent a spoon while scooping ice cream. It seems so silly to someone who didn't witness the event, but he was livid when I commented on his actions.

"For years, our disagreements were in the privacy of our home, shadowed by the dark sky of evening as discords emerged after dinner and a few stiff drinks. Then Val's behavior shifted, and what once was a private matter in our marriage became a public showing, at least with friends and family. He seemed oblivious or indifferent to the presence of other people, and his behavior became self-important and self-righteous, as though others weren't physically present. And he projected his emotions on his target, on me.

"One cold, wet spring when living in Jackson, we escaped mud season, the time of year the black-laced snow is quickly changing to water and the dirt beneath turns to a thick, sticky mud. We took a one-week hiatus and headed south to the warm, dry spring winds in St. George, Utah. We rented a quaint adobe-style home in Kayenta, a unique, tranquil community surrounded by red cliffs and steeped in cultural history. Midway through our stay, we invited two couples over for morning golf followed by afternoon drinks and dinner. Butch and Barb were good friends that had relocated from Jackson to St. George, and Ray and Sheelagh were staying in Mesquite, Nevada, in their getaway home.

9. Nakken, *The Addictive Personality*, 47.

"It was an exceptionally hot day for May—110 degrees—and we were sweltering in the heat after our midmorning golf outing. The desert willows and bottlebrush provided plenty of shade for us. We pulled the patio rocking chairs into a tight circle, extending our arms out and lifting our faces to the sky so our hot skin could lap up the moisture from the overhanging misters as we sipped on cold beers and shared stories about the best and worst golf shots.

"A few beers later, I prepared an early dinner of melon and mozzarella balls wrapped in prosciutto, pan-fried potato pancakes, BBQ ribs, and salad. The kitchen in our little rental home was small, and I had pots and pans covering the blue-tiled counters. Leaving all the dishes behind, we sat down at the outdoor, rustic pine table and enjoyed our mouth-watering ribs after we let the meat fall off the bones, stabbing the soft meat and taking sauce-drenched bites. We talked for an hour before I excused myself to take dishes into the kitchen to begin the cleanup duty. Barb joined me, and we visited as I dunked plates in the soapy sink water, then handed them to her to place in the dishwasher. As we continued, I caught sight of Val out of the corner of my eye—he had come into the kitchen and was standing beside me.

"He walked past Barb as though she were invisible and with disgust and intensity said, 'Why aren't the dishes done? What have you been doing in here?'

"I was shocked. He had never taken issue with meals or cleanup. Dumbfounded, I calmly replied, 'Barb and I are cleaning the kitchen. We will be back to the patio in fifteen minutes.'

"'You are such a stupid bitch! How long does it take you?' he yelled, staring at me, unaware that Butch was walking up behind him.

"'Hey, Val,' Butch said, reaching out to take his arm and turn him away from me. 'Why don't we go for a swim and cool down. It would be good for you to jump in the swimming pool and relax.'

"'Sure, let's go.'

"Butch and Val walked outside to the front patio, past Ray and Sheelagh, and disappeared around the corner of the house to the swimming pool. Val walked past Ray and Sheelagh as though they were invisible and weren't sitting on the patio in front of the kitchen bay window listening to Val's outburst. He was indifferent to other people, oblivious to their thoughts and reactions. He was self-absorbed!

"I was so embarrassed. Barb told me the heat and too much alcohol had made him reactive and to not be embarrassed; we were all good friends. Ray and Sheelagh said nothing. It became apparent to me that our friends had noticed the changes in Val's behavior and were aware of his addiction."

"Thank you so much for sharing with me, Kym," Judy said. "I am often reminded that when the addictive personality takes hold and the Self is no longer in control, the person feels sorry for themselves and they look for someone else to blame as the bad guy—that someone is usually close—and that person was you. I hope you realize you were not responsible for his behavior and you could not have altered the event."

Judy checked her watch and said, "Let's meet for coffee again, maybe tomorrow or the next day, and continue our conversation. I am also hoping you will take the time to locate and attend a nearby Al-Anon meeting. You may find solace in knowing others have had similar experiences, and it will be helpful to learn how life with an alcoholic has changed them as well as you. It's something to think about."

We put our coffee cups in the dish bin and left the cafeteria. At the doorway, Judy gave me a gentle, loving hug and said, "Take care of yourself and get some rest. You have been living for two people for too many years."

"I will, and thank you."

I walked out into the warm sunshine and smiled. I thought, *I like Judy. I will call her The Hug Lady*! A hug was just what I needed.

CHAPTER 11—STICKS AND STONES

A relationship with an active addict is extremely painful and emotionally dangerous. In the addict, there are two personalities—the authentic self and the addict. The addict does not care about friends or family or even the self. The addict begins to project their addictive values—negative values, which are mistrust, suspicion, and blame—onto others. The addict is delusional and reacts to friends and family who try to address the problem drinking with a defensive mechanism. I often endured this senseless verbal abuse. Here are some Val phrases from my journaling:

You suck as a partner and friend.
You are a freak just like your parents.
I can never talk to you.
You don't support me.
You don't defend me.
You always defend yourself.
You make me feel alone. You ignore me.
Are you trying to make me crazy?
You are a worthless bitch! You make me sick.
Go take another nap; you are so worthless.
You are a dumb bitch; I should break your knees.
You make me want to hit you.
Look at you, all pissed off. Are you going to cry?
Get out of my sight before I hit you.
The things I used to find cute about you now annoy me.
Can you just not speak!

Are you really that stupid to say something back to me?
If you say one more word, I will pound your face in.
Just shut your piehole!
I am done with you.
Little Miss Piggy.
You are like being married to an old hag.
You promised, "Until death do us part."

CHAPTER 12—A CLEAR BLUE DAY

DAY 6. Almost a week had passed since Val was admitted to the ICU. It was 10:00 a.m., and I had just arrived at the hospital. I walked into the ICU, and the lead nurse told me that Val was still hallucinating and drifting in and out of reality, though reality was a small beam of light in a dark cloud of confusion. He had endured another bad night, repeatedly demanding to be released, insisting to the night shift nursing staff that he was better and could go home, pleading that he had stopped drinking and smoking and promising he would never drink again.

When he had not gotten the response he'd wanted, he had behaved like a spoiled child. He had waved his cotton-padded, mittened hands up and down as far as the restraints would stretch. Then he had raised his faint and hoarse voice, pleading with the nurse that he had rights and couldn't be held against his will.

The nurse had calmly repeated the same truth, said probably a hundred times over the past week—the truth that he was sick and could not go home yet. Moreover, he had too many drugs in his system. When the nurse had finished speaking, Val had protested again, telling him that he would go home for just fifteen minutes and then come right back. He just wanted to see his home and his dog.

As the nurse told me about Val's evening, I thought that, in a way, he was a prisoner in the ICU. He had admitted himself of his own volition, but now he had no choice other than to receive medical treatment. After all, he was in a life-or-death situation.

I walked into Val's room, surprised to find him awake. He was not sedated. I looked at him and smiled. "Good morning. How was your

95

evening last night?"

He attempted to push himself upright in the bed, and with a look of fright in his eyes, he said, "You have to get me out of here. They hit me last night and pinned me down again."

I could see in his eyes he believed that he was in danger. He believed the hallucinations. I tried to reassure him by responding, "Val, I am sure they did not hit you. It takes two nurses to grab ahold of your arms and lift you on the bed. Maybe you thought they were being rough with you."

He snapped at me, "You don't believe me. They hit me and pinned me down in the bed."

"I am sure they weren't trying to hurt you. You are in a hospital. Nurses don't hurt patients."

"You don't believe me. Do you know what else the nurses do? They stand around all night, laughing and partying. I yell that I can't sleep, and they ignore me."

"Val, you are having hallucinations."

"I am not. You never believe me or defend me. You are nuts."

I did not respond.

I had spent the last decade, maybe two, trying to rationalize with an alcoholic. I had finally learned my lesson—I could not help Val with his alcoholism or his hallucinations.

I reached out to hold his cotton-padded, covered hand and said nothing. He looked at me with bewilderment and anger in his eyes. I thought, *His eyes were such a striking medium blue. I used to buy him marine-blue dress shirts because the color made his eyes sparkle. Now his eyes are sullen and a grayish blue. No sparkle. They show no remorse or understanding of what he has done to himself or me. They are lifeless.*

He repeated his demand: "Take me home. I am better."

I explained, "You are not yet well enough to go home."

He became angrier, telling me with his eyes that I was betraying him. The demands and protests went on for hours. He never tired or slept. He would occasionally be calm for fifteen or twenty minutes, saying nothing, then start the demands again.

I stayed at the hospital most of the day, leaving briefly to have dinner. I returned by 6:30 p.m. Val had been sedated again and was on a ventilator. I looked around the hallway for a nurse so I could ask what had happened while I was gone. As I waited for a nurse, I thought, *The pulmonary doctor must have visited Val while I was away and determined that Val needed to be on a ventilator.*

I continued to wait. The nurse night shift started at 8:00, and the day shift nurses were summarizing their notes and leaving patient information for the next shift. The comedic nurse, Paul, had moved aside the ugly turquoise chair and rolled in an extra nursing chair—a comfortable office chair with back support. I sat in the office chair and used my feet to roll the chair up to the left side of the bed. I placed my left hand on top of Val's left hand and held it. The nurses had removed the cotton-padded mitten restraints from his hands; I was careful to avoid squeezing his bruises. I caressed his hand and forearm. I told him I was in the room with him.

I sat holding his hand for a few more minutes. Paul entered the room and greeted me with his usual eagerness. He asked how I was doing and then told me what had occurred in room 442 while I was gone.

Paul pulled up Val's blankets and adjusted his pillows as he explained, "His oxygen level was dangerously low, and he wasn't compensating on his own. The pulmonary doctor decided to sedate him and place him on a ventilator. We currently have the oxygen turned up to the highest level; his oxygen saturation is only 61 percent, and his blood pressure kept spiking to 160 or 180. We are in a wait-and-see mode. He is fighting for his life."

I did not have any questions. I did not know what to ask. Val was extremely sick, and the nurses and doctors were trying hard to help him. Paul left the room, and I sat for a few more minutes. I felt numb. Helpless. I listened to the sound of the ventilator as it pumped oxygen into Val's lungs. The monitors made a four-part sound, much like someone ringing handbells, each with a slightly higher pitch, when the activity of the oxygen or heart displayed abnormal, or outside of the normal range. Every time the bell rang four times, I turned and stared at the display. I worried about what was happening. Was his oxygen dropping? Was his blood pressure spiking? Was his heart beating? I hated the handbell ringer.

I put Val's limp hand down and pushed my chair back as two nurses came into the room to check his vitals, replace some IV solutions, check the oxygen tank reading, and monitor Val's breathing. Their movements, a rhythm much like birds in flight, moving side to side in unison, became more rapid, checking the monitors more frequently. Their silent concern and increased movement led me to ask without hesitation, "Should I leave the room?" Intuitively, I knew something was wrong. Val's vital signs were changing for the worse.

One nurse said, "Yes, please wait in the hallway." She moved faster and more deliberately. I quickly got up and went to the nurses' station just outside the room. The nurse pulled the curtains closed behind me. The center of my chest, below where the rib cage comes together, began to pulsate. A rush of warmth flooded me, and the hallway filled with a piercing, intense command: "CODE BLUE 442, CODE BLUE 442."

The sound echoed in my mind as I watched medical teams come from two different directions and rush into Val's room—room 442. One team from my left had a crash cart and equipment to perform CPR. The team on my right, not rushing but moving quickly with purpose, had several small ice chests on pull carts. I thought, *Most likely the organ donor team.* Val was an organ donor.

I had to move. I could not stand outside his room. I was afraid of what was going to happen over the next few minutes. Tears flowed from my eyes as I wandered to the other side of the ICU. I searched for a social worker or another nurse to talk with and console me. It seemed everyone was in room 442.

This side of the floor was quiet, and no nurses were sitting at the desks. I sat in one of the nurse's chairs and waited. A minute, maybe two passed. I could not see or hear any of the commotion in room 442. I was anxious and stood up to pace. As tears flowed down my cheeks, I unexpectedly looked up to the ceiling. In an instant, I was aware of three sources of energy: the one inside me (my spirit) and one to my left and one to my right. Those beside me were rising from the level of my shoulders and moving toward an apex to meet in the center above where I was standing. The energy made the shape of a triangle, with me standing squarely in the center.

The energy outside of me had no light, no color, yet I could sense the movement of space in two linear lines moving together to the apex in front of me. I knew the energy was spiritual. My spirit in the center, Val's spirit to my left coming from room 442, and a Divine Spirit to the right, coming from behind my right shoulder. I sensed that the Divine Spirit to my right was sent to show Val the way to heaven. To welcome him. To offer him God's grace and take him to a peaceful, pain-free, and beautiful place above our human earth.

The purpose of the Divine Spirit was clear. In three seconds, maybe five, I communicated with each spirit. It was not a conversation of words, and it was not a linear conversation that we have when we are speaking to one another, but simultaneous. A conversation is probably an incorrect description, but it is how I can explain it given how we as humans communicate. It was an immediate understanding between the two spirits—one still earthly and the other heavenly—and the witness, my spirit.

I continued to look up toward the apex of the energy flows and, without speaking, communicated that my husband was in the hospital for his heart and alcoholism. He was in intensive care to get better, not die. Val's spirit communicated that he needed more time—he wasn't ready. The Divine Spirit communicated approval and agreed that he would stay. The energy sources instantly dropped back down past my sides. The energy inside my chest lowered from my head to my gut and slowly dissipated.

I sat and waited. What had just happened had lasted no more than five seconds. My mind felt numb. I sat wondering if Val had died. I sat for another minute, waiting for someone to tell me the ending to my spiritual connection with Val and the Divine Spirit. And then so many visitors entered my guesthouse: sorrow, anxiety, anticipation, fear, and anger.

Judy, the social worker, came around the corner to find me, her face devoid of the kind, calming smile she always had during our shared cups of coffee. I feared Val had died, yet something inside me told me that he was still alive. She said, "They were able to revive him."

I said nothing.

She continued, "Let's give the nurses a few minutes before I take you back into the room."

I looked at Judy and thought, *Go to room 442. I will never forget that room number because "two" and "blue" are rhythmic. Rhythmic, like a heartbeat.*

Judy returned to room 442, and as I waited, I tried to pull myself together and wiped the tears from my eyes. I watched the organ donor team walk back toward me and past the Queen's Guard. Their pace was no longer hurried. They were talking casually and smiling—they were used to the ebb and flow of life; the code blue call was just another day in the hospital.

Another minute passed, maybe two. Then Judy returned and extended her arms toward me and gave me a hug. She asked, "May I get you something cold to drink?"

I replied, "No, thank you."

"Okay, hon. Are you ready to see your husband?" She said with a soft and kindhearted tone.

She gave my hand a strong squeeze and walked me back to Val's room. I felt apprehensive about entering. Almost scared. I took a deep breath and pulled the curtain panel to the right side as I walked into the room. I did not know what I was expecting to see, but he was lying in his bed, asleep. At least he appeared to be sleeping. He was in a medically induced coma. He was finally at peace—all those years of struggling with an addiction and now cardiopulmonary arrest—and unaware of all his internal pain and strife; he had been given a second chance at life.

The nurses explained that he had been given a paralytic drug and he would be paralyzed for twenty-four hours or more, until his body recovered from the trauma. A breathing tube was still down his throat, and a machine was keeping him alive. I stared at him for several minutes. Then the nurse told me to go home, to get some rest. "He doesn't know you are here, and you need to take care of yourself."

I took her advice, said goodbye to Judy, and left the room. I was exhausted and I had Brandy waiting for me. I turned and left through the Queen's Guard. As I walked through the lobby, my attention was caught by a book sitting by itself on a side table. I walked over to it and picked it up: *Proof of Heaven*. I tucked the paperback book into my purse and left the hospital.

Later that evening, I curled up in bed and began to read the paperback. The book is about Dr. Eben Alexander's near-death experience and how, while he lay in a coma, he journeyed beyond this world to the realm of super-physical existence where he met the divine source of the universe. After my recent experience with Val's near-death and my encounter with the Divine Spirit, I was captivated by Dr. Alexander's account. During his experience in a completely new world, he realized a beautiful girl was next to him, and without using any words, she spoke to him. He explains,

The message went through me like a wind, and I instantly understood that it was true. I knew so in the same way that I knew that the world around us was real—was not some fantasy, passing and insubstantial.

The message had three parts, and if I had to translate them into earthly language, I'd say they ran something like this:

"You are loved and cherished, dearly, forever."

"You have nothing to fear."

"There is nothing you can do wrong."[10]

As I read this passage, I realized my experience, when Val coded and I felt the presence of his spirit and the Divine Spirit, was similar. There had been no words, but I had understood the message—the Divine Spirit was granting Val time to remain on earth. And the message had blown through me with the same feeling of love and acceptance that I imagine Dr. Alexander felt.

---

10. Alexander, *Proof of Heaven*, 41.

Chapter 13—Al-Anon

DAY 7. Knowing Val was in a medically induced coma, I had the day to myself and decided to attend a local Al-Anon meeting. Al-Anon is a mutual support program for people whose lives have been affected by someone else's drinking. As I searched the internet for meetings in my area, I wondered, *Why have I waited until now to attend Al-Anon? I have known for years that Val is an alcoholic, so why wait until his health is in serious trouble? Until it is almost too late for him?*

I knew the answer. My husband monitored my time and activities. Joining an Al-Anon group in earlier years would have required that I lie about my whereabouts as I attended in secret. He needed control and power, and my attending meetings about alcoholism would deteriorate his control and increase his denial. Worse, if I had grown to find my intrinsic self and take hold of my life, foraging out on my own, he would have fought to keep his control—making my life and my family members' lives a living nightmare.

But now, Val was weak and I was in control of myself and my actions. I was on the PATH to Healing. I was not afraid and was undoubtedly ready to reclaim my freedom and my life. My personal well-being had been compromised; my internal candle's flame was dim, barely lit. Val would have to care for himself, attend rehabilitation, and get help through a support group—or he would wither and die.

There were several meetings that day in the greater Tucson area. I selected one in downtown Tucson. I drove downtown to the meeting held in an old, restored brick building—maybe an old schoolhouse. I entered and approached the help desk to ask for directions. The volunteer pointed toward the cafeteria and told me the meeting rooms were on the left side. I was running late and lengthened my stride to move quickly down the hallway. I reached the cafeteria and found the meeting room doors to my left. The first door did not have a sign with the meeting name, but the meeting room number was the number listed on the Al-Anon website. I opened the door, and ten heads turned toward me. I asked, "Is this Al-Anon?"

One man replied, "No, next room down the hall."

I closed the door and walked to the next door. I opened it, and the same ten heads turned and looked at me. Same meeting, different door.

The same man said, "One more door down."

As I closed the door, I felt embarrassed.

I opened the next door, and the room was packed. There must have been fifty people in the room. There were thirty or so sitting around tables placed together in a large rectangle, and another twenty sitting in chairs along the wall. I thought, *My God, there must be an enormous number of alcoholics in Tucson. Val is not the only one!*

The meeting had started, so I slipped into the room and found a chair along the back wall. The meeting leader was greeting the members and visitors, explaining that the group was a fellowship of relatives and friends of alcoholics who shared their experiences, strength, and hope to solve their common problems. "We believe that alcoholism is a family illness and that changed attitudes can aid recovery. Al-Anon has but one purpose: to help families of alcoholics. We do this by practicing the Twelve Steps and by welcoming and giving comfort to families of alcoholics. We will now read the Twelve Steps."

The meeting leader passed a piece of paper to the person on her left. A small, gray-haired lady in wire-rimmed glasses read aloud the Steps.

One: We admitted we were powerless over alcohol—that our lives had become unmanageable.

Two: Came to believe that a Power greater than ourselves could restore us to sanity.

Three: Made a decision to turn our will and our lives over to the care of God *as we understood Him.*

Four: Made a searching and fearless moral inventory of ourselves.

Five: Admitted to God, to ourselves, and to another human being the exact nature of our wrongs.

Six: Were entirely ready to have God remove all these defects of character.

Seven: Humbly asked Him to remove our shortcomings.

Eight: Made a list of all persons we had harmed, and became willing to make amends to them all.

Nine: Made direct amends to such people wherever possible, except when to do so would injure them or others.

Ten: Continued to take personal inventory and when we were wrong promptly admitted it.

Eleven: Sought through prayer and meditation to improve our conscious contact with God *as we understood Him*, praying only for knowledge of His will for us and the power to carry that out.

Twelve: Having had a spiritual awakening as the result of these steps, we tried to carry this message to others, and to practice these principles in all our affairs.[11]

As I listened to each Step, I thought about the meaning of Step One: *I don't understand how I am powerless over alcohol and that my life has become unmanageable. I am not the alcoholic. I manage my life simply fine. Shouldn't I be learning about the alcoholic and how I cope or communicate with an alcoholic?*
The gray-haired lady passed the piece of paper back to the meeting leader. Everyone thanked her for reading the Twelve Steps. The leader read the chapter "Step One" from *Paths to Recovery: Al-Anon's Steps, Traditions, and Concepts*. She then looked up at the members and invited volunteers to share their personal stories, using the questions at

11. "The Twelve Steps," Al-Anon Family Groups website.

the end of the chapter as a guide. She reminded us not to discuss the alcoholic but to share how each of us had been affected by an alcoholic and how we had dealt with our own experiences. She asked, "Who would like to go first?"

A large, jovial-looking lady in a colorful yellow-and-blue dress raised her hand. She said, "I would like to share my story about my granddaughter." She told us how her granddaughter, a beautiful, tall, thin young girl in her twenties, had abused alcohol for several years. The granddaughter had taken money from every family member and had stolen items from her house and sold them. She told us that she had learned to set boundaries and had told her granddaughter she was not welcome at the upcoming family birthday party. The family gathering was not going to be spoiled by her granddaughter's behavior. She explained how hard it had been to say no, but that it was necessary.

The audience thanked her, and the meeting leader asked for the next volunteer. Fifteen hands raised up high, and one by one, each person told their personal story. I sat and listened. I had experienced some of their narratives: their stories of being manipulated, embarrassed, and taken advantage of by the alcoholic. And now I had to set boundaries and learn to take care of myself—these actions are part of the Healing process on the PATH. Although I yearned to learn more about the alcoholic, it was an insightful meeting, and I realized it was the right time in my life to be attending Al-Anon. In fact, I would have benefited from going years earlier.

I was aware that it was my time to say no, my time to lessen the burdens of supporting an alcoholic and find myself—find peace and happiness.

I stayed for almost two hours. As the meeting adjourned, people gathered into small groups and continued to share stories. I joined one group and introduced myself as a first-time attendee. They welcomed me and encouraged me to share whatever feeling or experience was on my mind. In this setting, the group listened and then, if requested, shared similar experiences that helped put my experiences into perspective. They helped me begin to acknowledge and accept my reality as a codependent and helped me understand I was not responsible for another person's life and I couldn't solve my husband's life choices. I was not responsible for him. I was responsible for myself—I was responsible for living or not living my life. I mattered! It was time to become un-dependent.

After others shared their stories, one woman introduced herself as Martha and asked if I had questions about the program. I said I did and wanted to ask a bit more about the meaning of some of the Twelve Steps. I explained to her I didn't understand Step One: "We admitted we were powerless over alcohol—that our lives had become unmanageable." I asked, "How can I be powerless over alcohol when I am not the alcoholic?"

Martha smiled and replied, "You are a codependent who has let another person's behavior affect you, and you try to affect them by controlling or obsessing with 'helping' or 'caretaking'—taking responsibility for another's life. That other person in your life is an alcoholic, and he, your husband, is controlled by alcohol. His life is unmanageable, and therefore, your life is unmanageable. You can't change the alcoholic, and you can't overcome the effects of the disease by force or will or reason."

I replied, "I tried to control alcohol. My life has become directed by a bottle of whiskey—correction, hundreds of bottles of whiskey—and its effect on my husband's life. I must accept that I can't change the alcoholic. Step One is about giving up—surrendering to the truth that I am powerless over another person's drinking. But I am not powerless over my own life. I can make choices that meet my emotional, physical, spiritual, and financial well-being."

"And Step One is the bridge to Step Two," Martha replied. "Once you have admitted you are powerless over the alcohol, you begin to stop operating on self-will. You listen to others and receive direction from a Power greater than yourself—a Higher Power. Your Higher Power may be God, spirituality, a fellowship such as Al-Anon, or a collective of friends. It is something outside of yourself—greater than yourself. Steps One through Three are about giving up: meaning, stop operating on self-will."

I replied, "I have known for a while that I can't help or change my husband, but it is so difficult to let go and stop enabling the alcoholic—to stop being a caregiver. But my actions have to mirror that knowledge; I have to accept the reality and change my behavior."

Martha shuffled papers around in her manila folder and selected one page. She placed the sheet of paper on top of the folder and pointed to a hand-drawn diagram. She said, "Al-Anon was founded sixteen years after the founding of AA by Anne B. and Lois W. (wife of AA co-founder Bill W.). A historian[12] of AA discovered that some areas of the country held "beginners' meetings" where the Twelve Steps were divided into three classifications and taught in three short sessions to newcomers. This diagram groups the Twelve Steps into Steps One through Three, Steps Four through Nine, and Steps Ten through Twelve. The groupings represent changes you must make to work the Twelve Steps. Those changes are Give Up, Clean Up, and Live Up. The action you must take to Give Up is reaching out to others—accept that you are powerless over alcohol, and listen to others and receive direction.

"The action to take for Clean Up is self-knowledge. Feed your mind with information, and get down to the causes and conditions of your codependency. What codependent characteristics do you have: caretaking, repression, obsession, controlling, denial, or poor communication? Make a list of your moral inventory and then begin to solve your problems. Learn to depend on yourself, and stop abandoning your needs; wants; feelings of happiness, love, and self-worth; and everything that has compromised your life. Trust yourself. You can solve your problems.

"And the last action item comes with Live Up, and it is wellness. Take care of your mental, physical, and spiritual needs by continuing to take notice of your moral inventory, meditate, journal, and find a quiet space to relax and reflect. Detaching from codependency is about cherishing yourself—give yourself what you need."

I replied, "That makes sense, and I am beginning to understand how the Twelve Steps originally designed for AA members applies to the Al-Anon members who are the codependents of the alcoholics. The alcoholic and the codependent must accept their realities and then take responsibility to live their own lives, change what they can, and accept what they can't. I have been living a life of wash, rinse, and repeat. It is time to stop repeating my old patterns and behaviors. I must start down a new path to growth and change. My PATH to Healing."

I thanked the group for sharing, especially Martha, picked up some brochures, and left the meeting. I repeated, "Give Up, Clean Up, and

12 P., *Back to Basics*, 30.

Live Up. Give Up, Clean Up, and Live Up."

I thought, *That was a good support group, and the attendees had relatable poignant stories. I will attend more meetings. And, like many in the meeting who shared stories about detaching and setting boundaries, I too am detaching and setting boundaries.*

I had completed an application for an apartment a few months prior, and I was ready to sign a lease and tell Val he needed to help himself. And I needed to help myself.

CHAPTER 14—CROSSING A LINE

DAY 8. I went to the hospital that morning even though I expected to find Val unconscious. The intensivist greeted me and confirmed what the nurse had previously conveyed. He explained that Val had been temporarily placed in a comatose state with sedative medications—this is called a medically induced coma. He said, "Our goal is to protect his brain from further injury and give it time to heal itself. We hope that tomorrow we can reverse the coma and observe where he is in the withdrawal process. The heavier the drinker, typically the longer the withdrawal process. He is suffering hallucinations beyond the four or five days of the typical withdrawal range. He is unaware of his surroundings and will be unresponsive to external stimuli. Plan to come visit tomorrow, and if anything happens before then, I will be sure to have the staff call you."

I briefly stood by his side and then turned to leave for the day. As I was leaving, Judy was walking toward me.

"Hello, Kym. How is Val today?" she asked as she leaned in and gave me a reassuring hug.

"He is still in a state of paralysis," I responded. "He looks peaceful, pain free."

"Would you like to have coffee and continue our conversation? I want to know how you are doing and if our last talk was comforting."

"I would like that. Do you have time to go to the cafeteria now?"

"Sure." We turned and left the ICU. With coffee cups in hand, we made our way to the same private corner table in the cafeteria. I sat down and waited as Judy made her way back to the cafeteria line to purchase a cookie.

As she sat, she asked, "How are you feeling after our last conversation?"

"All right. I thought about the dinner party in St. George, and I admit I am embarrassed and ashamed for allowing Val to treat me badly. After that trip, I told him he needed to apologize to Ray and Sheelagh for his behavior and actions. Surprisingly, he did the next time we had dinner with them. However, as he began the apology, he confessed that I had suggested he apologize. He included me in his shame—as though I didn't have enough of my own!"

Judy pushed her bangs to the side and reminded me that addiction causes an abnormal relationship with everyone in the addict's life. She said, "In *The Addictive Personality*, Craig Nakken quotes Alcoholics Anonymous, '"Remember that we deal with alcohol—cunning, baffling, powerful!" This is also one of the most truthful ways to describe the emotional logic found in all addictions: cunning, baffling, powerful.'"[13] She turned to a section in the book and continued reading, "Addicts start to manipulate other people and treat them as objects. Not surprisingly, it doesn't make much sense to them that others are offended by this. The Addict is often very self-righteous and self-centered.'"[14]

She paused and smiled. "Kym, don't be embarrassed. Family members get caught up in the cog of alcoholism with the addictive person. Family members get entangled with the addictive person and they fight and try to make the addict more responsible, only to eventually withdraw, feeling frustrated and angry. And then when the addictive person's authentic self re-emerges, the family members try to reconnect, often feeling shame they had distanced themselves and weren't engaging with the addict. And together, the cog continues to rotate."

"Thank you for not being judgmental," I replied. "It is hard to accept all that I have done to perpetuate Val's addiction or at least his using me to continue, if not deepen, his addiction to alcohol."

Judy took a bite of her warm chocolate chip cookie and asked, "I know you feel used, but when do you think he became dependent on you, or at least thought he could exploit you?"

I hesitated a moment, then replied, "The dependency started early in our relationship. I knew Val's father was a mean-spirited, verbally

---

13. Nakken, *The Addictive Personality*, 9.
14. Nakken, *The Addictive Personality*, 47.

abusive man who left deep scars in Val's self-confidence. I always wanted to help build his self-confidence, and instead of giving him positive feedback for accomplishing things on his own, I would act, with his approval, and accomplish things for him. It started small, letting him copy a college report or finishing his computer lab work when he didn't understand, and then my meddling became more significant. I prepared a business plan and found investors to help him buy a mail-order water-sports business. When the mail-order business closed due to vendor constraints, I created projects for him in my consulting practice. I didn't let him develop self-confidence on his own, and he learned that I would always be there to fix life's problems. Worst of all, I believe I contributed to deepening his lack of self-esteem. For the addictive personality, I was a sure bet! The addict could use me to deepen the addiction."

Judy wiped a little spot of melted chocolate chip from her lip and said, "Most people don't realize for a long time that they are dealing with an addict, not to mention that most people don't know how to effectively deal with an addict. Don't be so hard on yourself."

I nodded. "I guess. But there were so many years of pain and sadness, for both of us."

Judy paused and then said, "You mentioned that you enabled Val, but you were also a codependent, and codependents often don't know how to effectively deal with an addict because they haven't learned they can't change the addict. Just like you can't change Val. You have been so busy caretaking—thinking and feeling responsible for Val's feelings, thoughts, choices, and well-being—that you have forgotten to take care of yourself. You must detach, or disentangle yourself, from Val so you can look at your situation realistically and objectively. Detachment doesn't mean you don't care; it means you learn to care and be involved without hurting yourself. You must be responsible for yourself and let Val be responsible for himself. You can't solve problems that aren't yours to solve."

"You are right. And I also know he is responsible for his recovery."

"Yes, if he chooses to recover. And recovery doesn't lie solely in the other person. Recovery lies in you, in the ways you have let Val's behavior affect you, and in the way you have affected him with your obsessive helping and caretaking.

"Let's get back to your story about St. George. How did your life change after the St. George dinner party?" she asked.

"Gosh, things got worse. He became grandiose, and he continued saying inappropriate things to women." I sipped my coffee and continued, "We lived in a golf course community and would frequently attend dinner parties or have gatherings on the patio at the club house. Val started bragging to people how he was retired, pointing out that I liked to work and still had my consulting practice. But worse, his inappropriate comments toward women became very bizarre—creepy.

"One snowy winter evening, we were at Ray and Sheelagh's cabin for a dinner party. One of the guests, Patti, was serving appetizers, and the top button on her blouse had popped open. Val noticed and told her that her boobs were showing. Patti handled it well and buttoned her top button. Later that evening, the guests had moved outdoors to the back patio, where a few were enjoying a cigar while the rest of us sipped an after-dinner drink. Patti was mentioning that she had had her hair recently cut and colored at a new salon in town. Val interrupted her and asked her husband if the carpet matched the curtains. She was so angry that she got her coat and her husband and they left the dinner party. Val acted as though nothing had happened. He didn't respond to her reaction. He didn't apologize to Patti, or to Ray or Sheelagh, and he said nothing to me. He was in his own world—his own perception of reality, a complete disconnect to social or behavioral right and wrong."

Judy shook her head. "Addiction is perplexing and frustrating for the family." She then pulled *The Addictive Personality* from her purse. She thumbed the pages, stopped on a highlighted page, and paraphrased: "The addictive person feels like a stranger within themselves. The person feels anger, fear, and pain. The Self personality turns to the addictive personality for comfort. The pain and anger fuel the addictive process—deepening the addiction." She continued, "Remember, the addict is often self-righteous and self-centered. And, like your husband, Val, addicts make statements like 'I am retired' that support the addictive process and belief system—it gives them comfort."

I shrugged my shoulders. "I guess. He made comments at dinner parties until, eventually, we were no longer invited. His behavior affected my friendships and social gatherings. It wasn't long after our isolation—which is not easy in a close-knit, gossipy golf community—that Val's behavior at home became more bizarre. His anger became directed toward me, but, interestingly, it followed a pattern, a ritual. I would go to bed at 9:00 p.m. because I worked all day and was an early riser. He would stay up, often telling me he would be to bed in an hour. I would be asleep, and at 10:00 p.m., he would enter the bedroom, flip on the light, and gruffly ask me why I went to bed without saying good night. It was as though he lost an hour of time and then suddenly snapped back, realizing I wasn't in the room, and he would come searching for me. I believe he was probably blacking out. Of course, I used intellectual logic and explained I had kissed him good night an hour ago and had gone to bed. He, using his emotional logic as you have explained to me, would start yelling at me and ask me if I was trying to make him go crazy. Or worse, he would call me a freak for going to bed early."

Judy put her hand on my shoulder and gave me a small, reassuring smile. She said, "It appears Val was toward the end of the Crucial stage of alcoholism; he was displaying memory blackouts, aggressive behavior, and loss of ordinary willpower, not to mention impaired thinking. This is also referred to as Lifestyle Change. Craig Nakken explains that pain and anger fuel the addictive process, and both pain and anger are real to the addict and those who surround them."

I gazed at Judy and put my hands to my cheeks. "Judy, it was like living in *The Twilight Zone.* I couldn't respond to him because it would agitate him more. Sometimes, his legs would start quivering because he was so tense and volatile. I had to tolerate his outbursts or face the consequences of addictive logic. The rage in his eyes made his feelings undeniable, and I feared him acting out."

Judy held my hand. "Honey, were you safe? Did he hurt you?"

I squeezed her hand too and began explaining how I lived in fear of being controlled, including physical control; I lived in fear of the unknown. "He would tell me I made him feel as if he wanted to choke the life out of me. He would push me or hold me facedown in my pillow. Curiously, he never hit me with his fists. I remember him telling me a story about when he was a young boy and his mom took him on errands. One day, she wore big, round, dark sunglasses into the dry cleaners to pick up the laundry because she had two black eyes. Val's father was an active alcoholic at the time and had beaten her. Val never forgot how he felt, sitting on the counter at the dry cleaners, watching his mom pay her bill and wearing those big sunglasses."

I paused.

"His verbal abuse was illogical, and it frustrated me that I could not rationalize with him—it is my nature to sit quietly and say nothing. Val's blackouts and bizarre evening behavior prompted me to keep a journal in my nightstand. After frightening episodes with Val, I would take out my journal and, in the dark, write about the events. I didn't know if I was keeping the journal to prove to him that he was an alcoholic, or to remind myself I had cause to detach myself from him. Regardless of the purpose, I journaled for a decade until last year when Val's health failed and he no longer entered my bedroom at night. I still have the journal, and each entry reminds me of his irrational behavior, name-calling, and meanness.

"One evening, I lost my self-control. He entered the bedroom around 10:00 after I had fallen asleep. He stood just past the open doorway, holding on to the curved door handle, and he started yelling at me in protest that I had left him alone on the couch, telling me that I made him feel lonely and that I was a terrible partner and wife, a worthless wife. He started to turn back toward the hallway, continuing his rant with a few interjections of 'bitch,' and I thought, *I am the terrible partner*, and in an instant, I was filled with rage. I threw the blankets to the side and pushed myself out of bed while grabbing the nightstand lamp. I placed both hands around the square base and heaved the solid shaft across the back of his head. He lost his balance and fell against the bedroom door, only to regain it and move toward me with the soft glow of hallway light framing his rage. I raised the lamp above my head and crashed it down again, hitting his neck. He started to make a fist, then stopped and left. I watched him walk away stiff-legged and jerky, not quite a stagger. I was lucky he didn't kill me that night. And for a moment, it didn't matter to me if I had killed him. I was so full of malice—a dark and ugly visitor I had not welcomed into my guesthouse, but had, nonetheless, appeared.

"And the lamp, it tilts but it sits on my desk as a reminder of life with an alcoholic and how that night I crossed a line. I had relinquished my intellectual thinking to frustration, to anger, to rage. My behavior was mirroring Val's behavior as I became further entangled in his alcoholic web. I was deep on the PATH of Anger. I had so much Anger!

And yet it is painful for me to accept responsibility for my actions in our shared dysfunction."

Judy continued to hold my hand, and we slowly finished our coffee.

CHAPTER 15—LUCIDITY

DAY 9. Almost two days had passed with Val in a coma. Every part of his body had been still since he had coded. When I entered his room, he was lying on his back with his head tilted to the right, his waist slightly bent to the side, and his hands lying flat on his stomach. His eyes were closed and his face was relaxed. He looked so peaceful, yet lifeless. I was told he wasn't aware of external stimuli, but I wondered if maybe he could sense me holding his hand; talking to him—telling him how he had briefly died but the medical team had revived him; touching his face and telling him about my experience with his spirit and the Divine Spirit; and asking him if he could remember the brief journey toward heaven and his communication with the Divine Spirit.

During his coma, the hospital staff took a CT scan of his brain and chest. Neither scan revealed any internal bleeding or other issues. His systolic blood pressure, the top number that measures the force of blood against the artery walls and an important number to the medical staff, was holding steady around 120. His oxygen level was at 100. His temperature was 102.6, better but still too high. His body was still unable to compensate on its own.

Then, it was time to stop the IV drip with the paralytic medication while slowly reducing the sedative. It was time to slowly awaken him.

As he awoke, he struggled with the intubation—fighting the tube in his throat that allowed oxygen to pass into his body. He slowly accepted the tube and became more lucid. The nurse told Val the tube would stay in until his blood pressure dropped below 120. His blood pressure had dropped from 180, the value a few days before, to a range within 120 to 130. But it had to get lower.

He looked at the nurse as she spoke, but his look was expressionless. I didn't know if he understood or, worse, cared.

I spent the next hour holding his hand, telling him he was going to be all right. The Divine Spirit had given him a second chance to live.

He was unresponsive.

I sat and waited for him to awaken. About an hour passed, and I felt him gently squeeze my hand. I looked over to his face and saw that he was looking at me; his eyes looked confused and full of questions. He tried to speak but nothing came out. He swallowed and tried again. This time he uttered a faint whisper. His words seemed to cling to the tube in his throat, so I leaned my head forward, tilting my right ear next to his mouth, reaching to hear his words. He whispered again, and I shook my head no, telling him I could not understand him. He rolled his eyes backward in defeat. He relaxed his hand, letting go of mine, and closed his eyes. Saying nothing, I stood next to his side, gently placing my hand on his shoulder. I stood a few minutes longer, watching his chest rise up, fall back down, up, and back down as he slept. I left for the afternoon, planning to return after dinner.

Val was awake when I returned that evening. Tim was in his room and turned to greet me with a big grin. He said with excitement, "We have slowly reduced his sedative, and he is responding well. He seems to have made it past most of the detoxification and is more mentally stable, with no hallucinations to our knowledge. We are taking him off the ventilator tonight."

I replied, "That is good news."

Tim continued, "I have spoken to him again about his cardiopulmonary arrest and what he went through the past few days. I am not sure he comprehends what I am telling him, and he drifts in and out of sleep by the minute. I am hopeful tomorrow will be a better day and we can have another conversation. Really talk."

Tim turned directly to me and, in a softer but serious tone, said, "We were not sure he was going to survive. He is improving, but his kidneys did not produce much urine last night. The doctor has ordered a bladder scan, but we are waiting until we remove the ventilator." Tim walked over to me and gently touched my shoulder, then left.

I walked over to the chair, pulled it close to the bed, reached for Val's hand, and held it as he lay with his eyes closed.

At 8:00 p.m., Tim came back, clapped his hands together, and elatedly said, "It is time to remove the ventilator." Tim and another nurse gently removed the tape around the tube, then pulled the tube. Val squirmed a bit and coughed as the tube was being pulled out of his throat. He was struggling to make the transition from breathing through a tube to breathing on his own. After a few minutes, he was comfortably breathing. He struggled to speak; his throat was dry and irritated from the tube. He swallowed hard to wet his throat, then he tried again. Still, we could not understand him. I bent over, close to his face, and whispered, "Get some rest; your body has been through hell, and you must try to sleep." He looked at me bewildered and closed his eyes.

Breathing on his own made me feel at ease. He had endured cardiopulmonary arrest, a coma, and intubation. I hoped tomorrow would be a better day for both of us.

CHAPTER 16—A FLICKER OF LIGHT

DAY 10. I arrived at the hospital at 10:00 a.m. I was apprehensive about seeing Val, wondering if he would be calm or restless, rational or irrational, lucid or hallucinating. I walked toward his room; the curtains were drawn closed and two voices were bantering. It was the nurse, Tim, having a "come to Jesus" moment with Val.

Tim was sternly saying, "You have to stop drinking. It is pickling your brain, and you need to get off the booze. You will kill yourself if you don't stop drinking." He continued to tell Val that he needed to do something bigger than himself, something more important than himself, maybe volunteer at a soup kitchen, learn about people who were truly down and out.

Val responded, "I have volunteered with dogs. I could do that again."

Tim agreed. "It would be a good start. And you must enter alcohol rehabilitation."

Tim slid back the curtain and greeted me with a smile and a "good morning." He motioned his hand inward, inviting me in. I entered and looked at Val, and for the first time since his stay in the hospital, Val turned his head and gazed straight into my eyes. His hands, freed from the soft, white mittens, reached out for mine. I moved toward his bed and extended my hands. He grabbed hold of both and firmly clasped his fingers around them. He gently squeezed my hands as he pulled them to his chest. His eyes were clear and his gaze in focus. With the most sincerity I had seen in years, he said in a clear and strong voice, "I am sorry for not being a good husband. I am sorry for doing this to myself and you." Then he cried.

Until that moment, in the ICU his speech had been jumbled, faint, raspy, and enigmatic; his thoughts had been erratic, and he had been unable to focus on his dilemma other than to tell everyone, including me, that he had quit drinking and could go home. Now he seemed genuinely aware of his addiction and the toll it had taken on his life. He had asked the Divine Spirit for more time, pleading that he wasn't ready. And I understood. *He wasn't asking for more time for himself, but for time to acknowledge that he was an alcoholic and tell me he was sorry for his denial and destructive determination that deeply affected his life and mine. He had asked for time to apologize.*

I moved my hands, wrapping them around his, and said, "Val, you are not a bad person, but you have lost yourself to the alcohol addiction, and you need help."

He blinked and another tear rolled down his cheek.

I continued, "I forgive you for the denial and self-abuse with alcohol. You have been trying for years to slow your alcohol consumption, only to fail time and time again. Tim was just telling you, now is the time to renew your life by being truthful and connecting to yourself and to others with meaningful relationships. You will benefit from a Twelve-Step program. Without that commitment, I can no longer deal with your alcoholism and deteriorating health. I am no longer giving in to your alcoholism. I am going to help myself and do what is best for me—I am worth it. I am on my PATH of Healing."

Tears welled in his eyes and he blinked several times. Then he closed his eyes, and our moment of truthfulness and sincerity —a moment I will never forget— was gone.

I looked at the round clock on the wall, reminiscent of the large, bold, black-numbered clocks in grade school. I saw that it was time to meet Judy for her break.

She was reading a medical journal while she waited for me in the lobby.

"Some light reading?" I chuckled.

She put the journal down and stood to greet me. "Hello, hon. You look well rested today," she said. "The sun has set behind the outdoor garden; it might be cozy to sit outside."

"Yes, let's sit by the large willow boughs hanging over the small water ponds," I said, and we walked down the cobbled brick footpath to the distressed wooden gate that led us to peace and tranquility.

As we sat on the wooden benches, Judy set her sweater and books next to her and fumbled for her reading glasses. Finding them, she placed them on her face and looked up at me. "Now, tell me what happened after you realized your circle of friends and social events were changing as Val progressed further into addiction and the loss of his authentic self."

"Well, a lot happened that year," I said, shifting sideways on the bench to look at Judy. "After realizing I had crossed a line when I hit him, and, being at the apex of anger and disappointment toward Val's behavior and addiction, I had to take action for myself. I was married to a different person, and I did not like that person. I met with an attorney, and we drafted the paperwork, asset distribution plan, and other details necessary to file for a divorce. It was shortly after the 2008 housing crisis, and our assets were depleted, but I didn't care. In fact, he could have had everything if it had resulted in a divorce and peace for my mind."

Judy asked, "How did he respond when you told him you wanted a divorce? I imagine that he did not take it well since most alcoholics need to manipulate and use the people who have stayed in their lives. After all, you have made it easy for him to not work and to feed his addiction; you have enabled the addict personality to take further control. You cared about the authentic Val, his true personality, but the addict took over to manipulate and control you so he could fulfill his needs."

I nodded in agreement and said, "It is a bitter pill to swallow—acknowledging that I was manipulated again and again and again. And it didn't stop with the plan for a divorce, or I wouldn't be here at the ICU. After I left the attorney's office, I went home. I walked through the garage door to the mudroom, and as I bent over to take off my boots, I saw Val standing in the kitchen. He asked where I had been, and I told him I was visiting an attorney and wanted a divorce. The attorney would be filing the formal paperwork that week. I rehashed events of embarrassing episodes, pointing out friends who no longer invited us to dinner parties and how he drank a half gallon of whiskey every two days. In fact, I told him, 'You look forward to visiting the cashier at the liquor store and sharing stories—how pathetic.'

"His eyes teared up and he had an emotional meltdown. He begged me to stay, telling me he would stop drinking, get a job, and act right. He promised he would be a better husband. He told me I was his best friend and he couldn't be without me, that I was all he had. He pleaded like a child, and I gave in. It was my opportunity to enforce professional help or leave, and I squandered it. That day I learned to not make promises I wasn't going to keep. I learned that if you are going to set boundaries, you must know what you intend to do if those boundaries are crossed, and you must follow through with those intentions. Tell the alcoholic what the boundaries are and what the consequences are if the alcoholic crosses those boundaries. Remember to communicate— say what you mean and mean what you say. And don't communicate when the alcoholic has been drinking, or when you might have been drinking."

"And did he keep any of his promises?" Judy asked, raising her eyes and peeking over the top of her reading glasses.

I replied, "Oh, for a while. I foolishly agreed to give him time to prove he could refrain from drinking and get his life in order. I asked him to get professional help, and he refused—telling me he could do this on his own. He drank less for several weeks, and as he realized I was staying, his fear of losing me diminished and he went back to drinking more, although he wasn't going to the liquor store every other day.

"He tried hard for a year after I suggested filing for divorce. He started getting active—walking every day and working on home projects. And the intensity of his evening outbursts lessened, but mostly because we had agreed to sleep in separate bedrooms. In fact, he suggested we move somewhere warm—start fresh—and he would even get a job. He suggested the Florida Keys and was excited about the prospect of working in a marina or with a fishing guide."

Judy brushed her bangs to the side and claimed, "I know he didn't stop drinking, or, as you said, you would not be here in the ICU. Did he ever try to get professional help or attend an organization like AA? Once the addict is totally committed to the addiction and they have lost their authentic self, they can't free themselves without intervention."

"No, he never sought professional help. We did move to Florida, but only because of one last desperate act to control me so I would remain his caretaker. He used emotional blackmail to keep me in his life. Previously, I had stayed out of loyalty, friendship, responsibility, and hope that the authentic Val would return. Now I stayed out of fear."

"What do you mean, you stayed out of fear?"

I looked at my watch and reminded Judy that it was past her break. I said, "I will tell you about the fear next time we visit."

She hugged me and said, "Let's talk again soon. I think it is good for you to share some of those deeply buried stories."

CHAPTER 17—WIPE YOUR OWN ASS

DAY 11. I arrived at the hospital midmorning. I was surprised and delighted to see Val awake and sitting up in bed. Paul was in the room and was busy bundling IV tubes together and placing them on a hook next to the IV stand. He was preparing Val to move from the bed to a chair.

Val looked at me when I entered the room but did not express any interest that I was there. Paul pulled the blanket and sheet back, exposing Val's legs, his gown, and the catheter. Paul pulled his gown up to his stomach, exposing his groin. Paul then removed the catheter. Val winced and grunted as the catheter slipped free. Paul pulled Val's legs to the edge of the bed and then instructed Val to put his arm around his shoulder. Val obliged and Paul lifted Val's upper body off the back of the bed and sat him upright on the edge. He told Val to take a moment and gather his balance. Then, working together, Paul guided Val's feet down to the floor, and again, they paused. Then, in unison, Paul and Val stood up and shifted from the side of the bed to standing. Val wobbled slightly back and forth, but Paul kept hold of him and guided Val to the big turquoise chair. Val plopped sideways into the chair, but he was sitting. Paul straightened him upright and pulled his gown back down over his groin. He then fetched one of the oven-warmed blankets and placed it over Val's lap.

Almost two weeks had passed since Val had been in the ICU either strapped to a bed or lying motionless in an induced coma. Now he was awake, sitting upright, and seemingly coherent, though he resembled a dazed and confused boxer ready for a TKO. But he wasn't out yet! Dazed and a bit bewildered, but not out for the count.

He sat in that chair all day and into the early evening. He barely moved, occasionally glancing up at the television but not watching what was playing. He did not change the television channel or request something to watch. It just played one television program after another. I put some magazines on the stand next to the chair. I had bought a car magazine and a sports magazine so he could flip the pages and look at pictures without having to read and comprehend. He paid no attention to the magazines or the television. He barely looked at me. I sat and watched television, not paying attention either.

We continued sitting together in silence until the dinner hour. Val had been approved to have soft foods. He had not had soft food in almost two weeks, and he was looking forward to eating. A staff person brought him a tray of applesauce, orange juice, and yogurt. He looked at his dining choices and wrinkled his nose. He looked at me, and I knew he would not eat. He only ate applesauce with pork chops, and he didn't like yogurt. I opened the orange juice container and told him to at least drink the juice.

I stood up and walked out of the room and over to the nurses' station. All the chairs were empty, and I waited patiently for a nurse to return. Juan walked around the corner, and I smiled at him and waved him over to talk with me.

"What can I do for you, Kym?"

I replied, "Val will not eat the soft foods given to him for dinner. Are there perhaps some other choices?"

Juan grinned and replied, "Picky eater, is he?"

I nodded and smiled.

"I can give him some soft ice cream and Jell-O. Will he eat those?"

I nodded again and said, "Yes, he is a terribly picky eater, and yes, he will eat the ice cream and Jell-O. Thank you, Juan."

Juan slipped through a door, and I returned to Val's room. A few moments later, Juan returned with the ice cream and Jell-O. With a shaky hand, Val picked up a spoon and ate the Jell-O. Then he ate the ice cream. He seemed satisfied and fell asleep in the chair.

It was 7:00 p.m. and the nursing shift would take place in an hour. Before Paul's shift was over, he stepped into the room and asked how Val was doing and that he would help him back to bed. He looked at Val and said, "I hear you won't eat applesauce without pork chops? You are difficult, aren't you?" He smiled at Val and continued, "We need to get you back into bed, young man. But first, would you like to try using the restroom for a bowel movement?"

I don't think Val realized that he had not been out of bed for the past eleven days for a bowel movement. If he had gone, he had gone on a diaper sheet skillfully placed between the bedsheet and his bottom.

In a fatigued voice, he replied, "Yes, but I need help." Paul nodded and said, "Really? I thought you might pop right out of that chair and skip over to the toilet by yourself."

It took Val a minute to realize Paul was teasing him, and then he smiled. Paul helped lift Val out of the chair, and they slowly shuffled over to the toilet. It was in the corner of the room behind a tan-colored linen curtain. Val dropped down hard onto the toilet, but he stayed upright. Paul helped him regain his balance and then pulled the curtain shut and told Val he would be back in a few minutes.

It took Val about five minutes, but he was able to have a bowel movement. As I stood inside the curtain watching him, he put his left hand on the windowsill to balance himself and bent forward to reach for the moist wipes but could not touch the box that was on a stool in front of him. I stepped forward and gently pushed the stool toward him until he could touch the box. As he continued to steady himself with his left hand, he pulled a few sheets out of the box and tried to reach behind his back. He was unsteady as he struggled to reach behind. He turned and offered his hand with the moist wipes to me.

His defeated voice said, "Will you help me?"

I looked at the moist wipes and then at him and replied, "I am not wiping your ass. There are paid professionals here, and they can help you wipe your ass." I was surprised by my response. I felt a bit ashamed of myself for such a curt reply. I realized for the first time that I was telling him I had had enough of his nonsense, and going forward, he was going to take responsibility for his actions. I felt good. I felt strong. I felt relieved that I was letting go of being a caregiver. I was letting go of being a codependent.

He dropped his hand down to his lap and grunted as he exhaled. He tried again and managed to wipe himself. He tossed the soiled moist wipes toward the basket and missed.

I picked up the wipes and put them in the basket.

He whispered, "Thank you."

Paul returned to the room and was elated that Val had gone to the bathroom on his own. I told Paul I felt bad I had not wiped Val's bottom, and Paul snickered and said, "That is what we are here for, to help the patient. It isn't your responsibility. And, Kym, he is not a victim. He doesn't need you to fix things for him; he needs to take responsibility for himself and become independent in thought and action. He needs to learn you will not rescue him ever again. Kym—let go."

I smiled but still felt a little guilty for swiftly telling Val I wasn't helping him. I guess that was my clue that I was done taking care of all his problems. I realized I was done enabling him to be an alcoholic and done taking care of his ills. I had been a caregiver for so long, and I didn't need to take care of Val—he was responsible for taking care of himself. I was responsible for taking care of myself. I was on my PATH to Healing!

Val was back in bed, and I was getting ready to go home when the intensivist came into the room.

"How are you this evening?" he asked me.

"Tired. But Val had a good day and was able to sit in the chair and use the restroom," I replied.

"Good news," he said. "Now let's discuss the next steps. In a few days, if all goes well, Val will be released to the hospital's physical rehabilitation center. Once he is strong enough to leave the hospital, we are recommending he goes straight to a thirty-day outpatient alcohol rehabilitation center."

"It will be good if he does not go home before checking into a rehabilitation center," I said. "Given his distrust of professional help and group programs, as well as his distrust of anyone who does not drink, I am not sure he would ever check into a program if he went home immediately after the hospital."

"Agreed," the intensivist said. "Go home for the evening, and we will discuss it more as the time nears."

I agreed and picked up my purse. As I left the room, I thought about Val having told me earlier that day that he was never drinking or smoking again, and how proud he was of himself. But I no longer believed him or had any faith in his desire or ability to help himself. Drinking made him feel good; at least he believed it did. What had started as an illusion of confidence and joy, had eventually diminished his physical pain, the very pain that had developed from years of drinking. No, I didn't believe him. But I believed in myself. It was time to stop feeling responsible for his well-being and care about my own. It was time to lift the weight of his heavy hand off me and let him wipe his own ass.

This above all: to thine own self be true,
And it must follow, as the night the day,
Thou canst not then be false to any man.
—Shakespeare, Hamlet

CHAPTER 18—DETACHING

DAY 12—morning. As I left my neighborhood, I didn't drive toward the hospital. Instead, I turned in the opposite direction and drove toward my future temporary home—a home without Val. As I drove, I thought about our last visit to Mayo Clinic: that evening he confessed to me his love for alcohol, and I knew he was never going to stop drinking or go to a support group. By mid-July, he was still taking oxycodone and drinking whiskey—pouring for himself fifteen ounces a night instead of twenty ounces, a dismal scorecard. I recalled a conversation we had one morning in July as I sat on the couch across from his glare and said, "I went to look at an apartment—I am moving. You are never going to quit drinking, and I can't help you with doctor appointments and all your health issues if you do not help yourself. I have spent too many years trying to help you, and it was not my place—you are responsible for your own actions. I can no longer be part of this relationship. I feel empty. Used up."

Tears rolled down his cheeks as he pleaded, "Please don't leave me. I know you no longer love me, but please stay as my friend. I have no one." He was right; he didn't communicate with his brothers, and he had alienated some of his friends. Having no one to help with his physical deterioration had left him a danger to himself and others.

I nodded and said, "You used to be my best friend. You have taken that away from me, from us."

Tears continued to roll down his cheeks, and as he pulled at the bottom of his T-shirt, he said, "I know."

"I will stay as your friend," I replied apathetically. I lied. The next day I took the completed application back to the apartment office.

Now, two months later, it was September and I knew staying in my home was not possible; the admission of Val's true love was a pail of water thrown in my face. Had I known he was an alcoholic? Of course. Should I have made this decision years earlier? Probably, but the progression of alcoholism and the impact on the family is a painfully slow process—taking family members with it into the web of alcoholism: Pre-Alcoholism, Early Alcoholism, Crucial Alcoholism, and Chronic Alcoholism. Detangling from the web is complicated, especially when the spider is suspicious and resentful. A wrong move in the web, and the consequences can be devastating.

It was time to leave the web.

I arrived at my destination, pulled into the parking lot, and parked in the visitor's stall. I looked up at the sign and read, "Welcome to your new home." A wave of sadness flooded me. I had not lived in an apartment since graduating from college. I thought, *I am starting over.* And then I reminded myself, *It is temporary. Get a divorce and then decide where you want to live, buy a house, and move on with your life.*

I was done Tolerating on my PATH.

I walked to the office, where I was greeted by the office manager. I informed her I was ready to select an available apartment and move in. We walked around the complex and visited the four available units. I selected the one closest to the pool. Though it would be loud with music and sunbathers, I wouldn't feel alone surrounded by people who were enjoying themselves.

The office manager and I returned to the office where I signed the remaining paperwork and collected the apartment keys. I left the office and headed home. It was time to pack the basics and prepare for Val's eventual return home.

I pulled into our home driveway five minutes later. I thought, *Perhaps I should have found an apartment farther away. It might be a problem to live so close to Val while he is dealing with substance abuse. To add to his ordeal, divorce papers will be served. Val will blame me for his actions and tell me I am not abiding by my wedding vows—And in sickness and in health . . .* The spider keeps its prey in the web with manipulation, blame, and guilt. The spider needs control so it can have power, because power removes insecurities and self-doubt—power gives the illusion of being confident and secure.

I went into our house and walked slowly through each room, deciding what I was going to pack and take to the apartment. I then returned to the garage for several empty plastic bins. Taking them into the kitchen, I started filling each bin with necessities, adding to the first bin one towel, one pillow, one set of twin sheets, and one bar of soap. To the next few bins, I carefully positioned one frying pan, one pot, one set of serving dishes, spices, one box of cereal, one coffee canister, one jar of peanut butter, and one jar of jelly. I added the dog pillow and Brandy's food to the bin collection and carried each bin to the garage. I was ready for a quick escape—inevitable once Val was released to return home.

Stepping into the house from the garage, I heard the phone ringing. It was my aunt Jody. She knew I went to the hospital in the mornings and was most likely curious why I hadn't texted her to give an update.

I answered, "Hello."

"How is Val doing today?" she asked.

"I have not been to the hospital this morning," I replied. "I signed a lease for an apartment and just finished packing several bins. When Val comes home, I will be ready to leave."

"Will you do me a favor?" she asked.

"Sure," I replied.

"Will you take the guns out of the house?"

"I already took them to the neighbor's house. I took them over earlier this summer after finding Val sitting on the edge of the bed holding a gun in his lap."

"You never told me about that!"

"I know; there are a lot of things I have never told anyone about my life with Val."

"Okay, I am glad the guns are at the neighbor's house."

Her request did not surprise me. I assumed she was worried that Val would die from a self-inflicted gunshot wound if I left him and filed for divorce. It seemed like a reasonable concern that a recovering alcoholic would be depressed if he lost his wife and only support system. I was wrong. Later, my aunt would tell me she had been worried for *my* life.

CHAPTER 19—I SEE YOU

DAY 12—afternoon. It was Sunday, and the Seattle Seahawks were playing. Wearing my blue and green game colors, I arrived at the hospital about 1:00 p.m. A deadpan face and expressionless eyes watched me walk into the room. I sat down and put my right hand on his forearm, gently squeezing his arm and then his hand. "How are you feeling today?" I asked in a soft voice.

"I am all right," he replied. "I am tired and I can't sleep in here. The nurses are loud at night."

"What do you mean, 'the nurses are loud at night'?" I asked.

"They party all night in the hallway, and they snort cocaine. They drink and do cocaine all night. They ignore me when I try calling out to them—they don't respond, or they laugh at me."

"Val, I don't believe the nurses party. This is a hospital, and they are not allowed to have parties. They are here twenty-four hours a day to monitor and help patients."

"You don't believe me," he snapped. "You never believe me, and you never support me."

"I know, Val. I never support you . . ." I paused. "All right, Val. I will speak to the nurses for you. Meanwhile, let's watch the football game."

The Seahawks game was not being televised in our local area, so I flipped through the channels and found another game to watch. I glanced over at Val occasionally, and he wasn't paying attention to the game. He stared straight ahead at the wall or stared into the hallway. Most of the time, he stared into the hallway. We sat together for hours, saying nothing.

After the football game, I asked if he wanted to get back into bed and try to rest, at least close his eyes even if he could not sleep. He nodded, and I got up and walked to the nurses' station to request assistance. Tim was sitting at the nurses' station, and I asked, "I thought Val was past the detox stage and was no longer hallucinating? He told me all the nurses are partying at night and snorting cocaine."

Tim calmly looked at me, and with tender concern, he replied, "He is displaying continued withdrawal symptoms. He is anxious and unable to sleep no more than ten minutes at a time. Quitting drinking cold turkey and then having cardiac arrest has added undue stress to his body. The DTs have been prolonged."

"It has been almost two weeks," I said. "I thought it takes one week to go through the DTs."

"This is not a typical situation. Your husband is extremely sick, and his body and mind are struggling to compensate on their own."

"Will he ever get better?"

"I hope so. The cardiologist is concerned that there may be permanent brain damage."

"What can be done now to help him?"

"We have started him on Librium, which will help treat his anxiety and acute alcohol withdrawal. The Librium should help relieve the fear Val is displaying with the type of hallucinations he is having."

Saddened by the news, I gave Tim a weak smile and thanked him. "Val would like to go to his bed. Would you be able to help him?"

"Certainly. Let me find Juan, and we will lift him into his bed and get him tucked in with warm blankets."

"Thank you, Tim. Thank you for all you and the staff have done to help Val. I know he has been a difficult patient: loud, angry, and afraid."

I turned and walked back into Val's room. I sat next to Val, and we waited for Tim and Juan. When they arrived, I stood up, said goodbye, and left for the outdoor garden. I had plans to meet Judy for another visit. I left the ICU area and found Judy in the garden. Her eyes were closed, and her face was pointed toward the sky, inviting the sun to warm her skin. I sat down next to her, and she opened her eyes and said, "Hello, hon. How are you today?"

I gave her a gentle hug and replied, "I am all right. I feel strong and am making decisions for my own life—what is best for me. I signed a lease for an apartment and am ready to move when my husband returns home from rehabilitation."

"Good for you. It is your time to heal and take care of yourself."

"I am learning that lesson."

"Last time we spoke, you said you stayed in your marriage out of fear. Do you still fear Val, and would you like to share your story with me?"

"For the first time in years, I don't feel afraid. As Val has become weaker and feebler, I have become stronger and feel empowered to take control of my life."

"I sense he used power or manipulation to control you and scare you," she said.

"Yes." It was time to tell someone my deepest secret.

"In our last visit, I told you about filing for divorce but that I stayed. Our life was manageable for about a year, and then we decided we were going to start a fresh, new life. Val promised he would drink less and even look for work. We discussed options and decided to move to the Florida Keys. Val seemed energized and thought he could easily obtain work at a marina or with a boating or hardware store. Again, I believed him; I hoped it would be different this time.

"We finished packing all our boxes at the end of June. We hired a moving company in Jackson to move our furniture and boxes into a storage unit. We planned to keep the storage unit for a month while we visited friends and family in our home state of Washington before leaving cross-country to Florida. We would drive from Washington to Jackson to meet the Mayflower driver, load the moving truck and our van, and then make the long haul to the Southeast.

"The day the Jackson movers arrived, Val was finishing taping up the last of the kitchen items and I was mopping the hardwood floors. Val was taping box number fifty when the front doorbell rang. He lifted the box and turned toward the front door. He yelled in pain and froze. I took the box from him and helped him to the floor. He had had previous disc injuries, and he had just reinjured himself. He was in severe pain.

"Val was flat on his back and tried to relax while I assisted the movers. Four hours later, the movers pushed the metal ramp underneath the truck, pulled down the heavy metal door, and drove to our storage unit. The house was empty. No longer ours, it was time for us to vacate. I loaded our luggage into the van, and then I loaded the dogs. I went back into the house to help Val get up off the floor. He rolled to his side and then onto all fours. I held out my hand and slowly helped him to his feet. I held his hand and shouldered some of his weight as we made our way to the van. He was in agony, and yet, we started our drive to Washington.

"The drive took us two days. We stopped in Missoula for the first evening and arrived in central Washington the next afternoon. We had rented a small home for a month—a small, green house set back on a large grassy lot with old pine trees towering over the front lawn and home. The house was no larger than our first one-bedroom apartment. The front room had a small couch and chair with a square electric fan that was whirling around and blowing warm air. The U-shaped kitchen had plenty of counter space and new stainless steel appliances. The owners had left a bottle of Merlot and a welcome card at the end of the eating bar.

"The kitchen was diagonal to the open nook the owners had described as a bedroom. The bed was pushed up against the inside wall, requiring one person to climb to that side of the bed from the open side. The bathroom entry was so small the door would not open all the way. To enter the bathroom, you had to squeeze between the door and the bathroom sink. Once in the bathroom, you had to turn and face the sink and then sit. Then you were on the toilet.

"Val, the dogs, and I stood in the living room and looked at each other. It was too small, especially for someone with a back injury and nowhere comfortable to lie down flat, or have a separate bed to toss and turn in. We had paid for the tiny home for a month, and we would have to make it work.

"My aunt and uncle live in a small college town. Their two boys, both grown, also live there. The town is a good central hub for taking day trips to Seattle to visit one of Val's brothers and our friends. Our plan was to visit for a month and have fun golfing, attending family BBQs, and hiking. With Val's injured back, that was not going to be possible. I spent the first week visiting family without Val. Val visited the local chiropractor, whom he liked very much, and got some relief from his back pain. He continued to see the chiropractor for the second and third weeks, and then he had a restless night's sleep and woke up with severe back pain again.

"He could barely swing his legs over the side of the bed. He steadied himself by using the windowsill and pulled himself upright. I crawled out behind him and pulled his blue jeans from the chair. I held the jeans open in front of his feet and helped guide one foot into a pant leg and then the other foot. He tried to bend over to reach the waistband and pull up his pants. He winced in pain. I pulled his pants up for him and he zipped them. He lost his balance and sat on the edge of the bed. I brought his flip-flops over to the bed and placed them on his feet. The chiropractic office was closed for the weekend.

"I sat on the edge of the bed next to him and looked into his eyes. They had welled up with water, and I knew he was holding back his tears. He really hurt. I took his hand in mine and suggested we go to urgent care or the emergency room. He squeezed my hand. 'I hate doctors,' he said. 'But I need pain pills. I don't know if I can sit in a car and drive a half hour to the nearest urgent care. Let's go to the emergency room.'

"'All right,' I replied as I stood up and extended my hands out to help Val off the edge of the bed. He pulled himself upright and slowly moved one foot in front of the other as we walked to the van. He reached for the grab handle and pulled himself up while I pushed his butt up into the passenger seat, then closed the door.

"We pulled into the emergency room around 9:00 a.m. We repeated the same actions in reverse. He grabbed the handle and slowly slid down out of his seat while I guided his feet to the ground. He steadied himself, and then slowly we moved toward the entrance. His pain was undeniable.

"We walked into an empty waiting room, and I helped Val ease into a chair at the admissions desk. I sat next to him and helped him check into the hospital. We provided our insurance card and explained why we were visiting. Val completed a medical history form. The process was quick, and we were in an exam room in less than ten minutes.

"A nurse arrived and took Val's blood pressure and weight. She rolled the blood pressure machine back into the corner and then walked to the counter and laid down a booklet about smoking. She looked at

Val. With a disparaging tone, she asked, 'Would you like to discuss getting help to stop smoking?'

"Val and I were dumbfounded. He was in obvious pain, and she was inquiring about smoking instead of his back pain. I knew Val was going to be immediately irritated. He snapped at the nurse, 'I am not here to stop smoking. I know it isn't good for me. I am here to get pain relief.'

"She calmly replied, 'I will leave the booklet here, and you can leave it or take it home. The doctor will be in shortly.' She walked out the door.

"Val glared at me and snapped, 'I knew we shouldn't have come here. Doctors never want to help. They just want to tell you to quit smoking.'

"'Val, you are in pain and you need help,' I said calmly. 'You don't really have an alternative if you want help with the pain.'

"He laid back on the exam bed and bent his knees to take some pressure off his lower back. The doctor walked into the exam room and extended his hand to greet us. He introduced himself and asked Val to explain his back injury and previous history. Val obliged and told the doctor how he had first hurt himself in his late twenties kneeboarding and all the setbacks leading up to lifting box fifty in Jackson.

"'What are you currently doing for back exercise?' the doctor asked.

"'I am seeing a chiropractor, and it was helping until this morning,' Val explained. 'I am not a pill popper, but I need some pain pills.'

"The doctor looked pensive and crossed his right leg over his left. 'We will prescribe some pain pills. Also, you can help your back pain by getting more oxygen in your blood. If you stop smoking, it should help your pain.'

"Val raised his right hand in protest and said, 'I know smoking is bad for me. I don't need to be told to stop smoking. I need pain pills, and you have a responsibility to help me.'

"The doctor stared at Val. Then he asked the nurse to fill a prescription and give Val one tablet then. The nurse complied and brought Val a little paper cup with a pill and a cup of water. Val swallowed the pill. The doctor finished typing his notes and said goodbye.

"I helped Val off the exam bed as he snapped, 'Let's get out of here.' He grabbed on to my hand for balance and turned to leave the room—leaving the booklet behind.

"On our drive home, Val began ranting that I should have said more to the doctor about his back pain and that I should have defended him. I had just sat and listened. I had heard him tell me this so many times, it wasn't even worth a response. I was in the Tolerance phase on my PATH, and I tolerated his anger.

"We arrived at the tiny house. It was a hot day, but the large pine trees looming over the house kept it cool inside. The floor fan was whirling at high speed, and it was blowing air across the bed, which is where we found the dogs sleeping the day away. I told the dogs to get off the bed and then helped Val lie down on the bed, placing some pillows under his knees. It was early afternoon, and he spent the rest of the day trying to stay comfortable. The doctor had sent him home with a five-day supply of painkillers. The instructions were to take one pill three times a day for five days, take with food, and do not drink alcohol. Val wanted the pain to stop. He took another pill during the afternoon. At 5:00 p.m., he got off the bed and shuffled into the kitchen. He made a stiff drink of whiskey and 7UP.

"I protested. 'You know you should not drink alcohol with the pain pills.'

"He scoffed, 'The pain pills are barely helping. The whiskey helps the pain more than the painkillers.' He lifted his pink plastic cup to his puckered lips and swallowed a big gulp. He reached for the bottle of the painkillers that were on the counter next to the kitchen sink.

"'No, it is too soon to take another pill. This will be your third pill already, and it is only five o'clock.'

"'I need relief.'

"'I thought the painkillers weren't helping you.'

"He ignored me and steadied himself against the kitchen counter, unscrewing the cap to the bottle. He put a pill in his mouth and took another big gulp from his plastic cup. He used the counter for support as he walked out of the kitchen and over to the couch. He sat down with his big cup and continued to drink.

"I sat down in the chair beside the couch. I turned on the television and searched for a movie. I found one we both agreed to watch. We sat together, without speaking, and watched a movie. During the movie, I fixed some appetizers. He fixed another drink. We continued to watch the movie, and afterward, I cleaned up the kitchen. He fixed another drink.

"It was 9:00 p.m. I was tired and uncomfortable in the chair. Val was agitated, and he began to blame me for his back pain and making him visit Washington. He started blaming me for making him sell our house and move away from Jackson. He was slurring his speech and becoming irrational.

"'It is your fault we had to sell our Jackson house!' he yelled. 'Now we have nothing. Now we are having to move to Florida.'

"'The real estate market crashed. Why are you blaming me?' I said coldly. I should have kept quiet. He was mixing painkillers and alcohol, and I knew he was not rational. But I teetered between Anger and Tolerance on my PATH with an alcoholic.

"He stood up from the couch and walked into the kitchen. I took a few minutes before turning in my chair to peer into the kitchen. My lower jaw dropped, and I yelled, 'What are you doing? You can't take any more painkillers tonight!'

"'Screw you. You aren't the one in pain.'

"'No, I am not, but I am here to help you. You shouldn't take more pills.'

"'Leave me alone.'

"He took a pill from the bottle and popped it into his mouth. He washed it down with another swig of whiskey and 7UP. I just sat and stared at him. Then I made one of the biggest mistakes of my life.

"Visitors rushed through the front door of my guesthouse—meanness, outrage, and anger. I blurted out, 'I wish I never decided to visit my family in Washington with you. I wish I weren't moving to Florida with you. You promised me you would drink less, and look at you, mixing alcohol with painkillers. You are not the man I married. You don't even try to stop drinking. Your behavior is pathetic!'

"'You bitch!' he yelled.

"'I should have divorced you when I completed the paperwork in January of last year. I let you talk me into staying. Telling me you would cut back on drinking and smoking. Making more false promises.' I snapped. 'You never change, and you lie to me. I want a divorce.'

"His face turned red and his eyes turned dark. He became enraged, darted out of the kitchen, and lunged at me. I tried to stand up out of the chair, but he grabbed my shoulders. He pushed me across the room toward the bedroom nook. I stumbled and gained my balance. I stood and turned toward him in time for him to push me onto the edge of the bed. I leaned forward and sat up straight.

"'You bitch!' he screamed at me as spit flew from his mouth and his eyes bulged.

"'Stop it, Val. You have had too much to drink.'

"'You will never divorce me. You will never leave me. I will hunt you down and kill you and your boyfriend if you leave.'

"'I don't have a boyfriend, and stop threatening me.'

"Rage washed across his face—deep red, almost devilish. He raised his right hand and grabbed the collar of my black pajama top. He pulled hard and ripped it halfway down the front. Then he pulled down again and ripped the top open. I tried to stand, and he pushed me onto the bed. He grabbed my hair, pulling it to steer me to my side. He rolled me over onto my stomach and pulled my pajama bottoms down. I begged him to stop.

"He slurred, 'You bitch. You are never leaving me.' He forced himself on top of me, squeezing his thighs tight around my ribs, pinning me down even harder. He kept hold of my hair and pushed my face into the pillow, molding it around my face and forcing my warm breath to retreat into my nose. I took a deep breath, feeling my lungs expand but getting no air. I thrashed my arms, trying to hit his thighs, but it just made him squeeze his legs tighter. I gave up and I lay there. It was pointless to fight. It was pointless to yell or plea. And then suddenly, his body relaxed, and he rolled off me and fumbled his way off the bed. Saying nothing, he shuffled to the front door and slipped out into the cold night. I put on a new T-shirt and crawled into the bed. I slid to the wall side, and I turned and faced the wall. My eyes teared and I felt helpless. I felt afraid for my safety. I felt trapped. I kept silently repeating, *Please don't come back in and fight, please don't come back in and fight.* . . . Repeating it until I drifted to sleep.

"The next morning, I felt him next to me. I slowly opened my eyes but didn't move—not wanting to wake him and not wanting to relive last night's turmoil. Keeping my eyes on him, I shifted onto my back and adjusted my pillow. He opened his eyes. We stared at each other for a moment, and then without a word, he moved so quickly out of bed, grabbed my right arm, and used it as a rudder to navigate me onto my stomach. He pushed one hand into the small of my back; the other hand spread out like an eagle's claw, its nails digging into the back of my head. Like an uninvited guest, he rammed his way into me. I froze. He thrust back and forth with all his weight and with one purpose—to render me defenseless. Powerless! I kept my eyes shut and held onto the darkness draping my eyelids until he finished and his body weight shifted. Giving my head one more shove into the pillow, he released his weight and pushed himself off me. As he stood, he said, 'Oh, and happy birthday.'

"The message was clear. Stopping his attack last night and disappearing into the cold night air had been part of his plan. He had let the evening spill into the next morning when he would be clearheaded from painkillers and alcohol and he would be the dominator. I was hoping he had surrendered himself to the argument, but no, he had remembered it and had played his hand of cards—it was winner take all.

"My life was never going to be the same. I resented my husband, and I was afraid to leave him, fearful he would harass my family or, worse, find me and assault me. I had traveled down my PATH with an alcoholic and had navigated the twists and turns of rationalizing, getting angry, and tolerating his outbursts, to arrive at what felt to be the final curve in the PATH—turning inward and hiding my fears and feelings. I was experiencing yet another codependent characteristic—repression. I was deep into Tolerance on my PATH."

Judy put her hand on my arm and stopped me, saying. "Honey, I am so sorry he used physical power to control you. Did you share your story with a support group or a safety network? Did you seek professional help?"

"No, I never did," I replied. "Now I know the importance of seeking help: a counselor, Al-Anon, or a trusted friend. It is especially important since I was in an abusive relationship—I couldn't navigate the abuse alone—I didn't have the skills. Now years have passed since that day, and Val is in the depths of the late stage of alcoholism. He is a weak, broken-down person."

Judy continued to rest her hand on my arm, offering her reassurance and understanding. She said, "In *The Addictive Personality*, Val would be in 'Stage Three: Life Breakdown.' The late stage is a complete breakdown of life. To paraphrase bits and pieces from this stage, Nakken suggests it is in this lifestyle breakdown stage that the alcoholic behaves in ways they never thought possible. The alcoholic is totally committed to the addictive process and will not be able to break the cycle without some form of intervention. It is in this stage that the alcoholic interacts with others by manipulating and using them to fulfill addictive needs. Deep inside, the addict is afraid of ending up alone."

I nodded.

She continued, "I imagine that when you witnessed Val mixing pain pills and drinking alcohol and confronted him about leaving him, he knew he couldn't make you feel pity or guilt. He used emotional blackmail and created fear so you would stay."

I replied, "The manipulation worked. I never confided in any of my friends and family about that day. Yesterday, I told my aunt I was packing a few items so I could be ready to move to my apartment. She was intuitively concerned for my safety, and she expressed concern about the guns in our home. I eased her mind and told her the guns were at our neighbor's house. I didn't tell her I felt threatened by the guns; Val already had control over me. He had committed the unthinkable; he had selfishly raped his own wife so she would stay and allow the addict to live."

"How do you feel now? Does he still have control over you?" Judy asked.

"No. My safety was violated six years ago. We never spoke about it, and we never were intimate again—we have been sleeping in separate bedrooms and living separate lives, at least in our own minds. And now, Val is a weak, morally bankrupt, helpless man who clings to me with all his might—he has no one to help him but me. Ironically, or sadly, his downfall is my strength. He can no longer physically control me. I am feeling a surge of resilience, renewal, and purpose. I have a sense of freedom. I have started Healing on my PATH with an alcoholic."

I paused and said, "I see him. I see the man he used to be and the man he has become."

"And I see YOU," Judy said. "You are a strong woman, and you will heal. Healing is about allowing yourself to be who you are and accepting Val as he is. Healing is about identifying your behaviors that cause you problems and then accepting those problems and deciding what to do to learn new behaviors and devote yourself to taking care of you. Live your own life."

She leaned over and hugged me.

CHAPTER 20—GOOD NEWS

DAY 13. It was a cooler morning than usual for a September day in Tucson. I pushed the brew button on the coffee pot, attached Brandy's blue velvet harness around her, and set out for a long walk around the neighborhood. I had not seen many neighbors for the past two weeks, and many were out walking their dogs. Brandy and I greeted Lou and his dog, Wellington, and Cholpon with her dog, Shema. We chatted about the weather and the day's activities. No one asked why they had not seen me out walking. I think the neighbors knew Val was in the hospital and they didn't want to pry and ask about his health. That was fine with me. After two weeks of worrying, not sleeping, and eating little food, I was exhausted and emotionally drained. And I wasn't ready to openly discuss Val's alcoholism and all the damage his drinking had done to his body.

After Brandy and I had walked for an hour, we stepped through the front iron gate and into the house. I slipped her harness off, hung it on the coatrack, and went into the kitchen. The brewed coffee was cold. I poured a cup and put it into the microwave. As it heated, I poured a bowl of cereal. The microwave buzzed twice and I got my coffee cup, taking it and the cereal bowl into the bathroom, where I ate as I dressed to go to the hospital. I had already spent an hour with Brandy, and the morning was slipping away.

By midmorning, I walked through the Queen's Guard. The staff said good morning to me as though I were part of the family. As I entered room 442, I was delighted to see Val sitting up in bed and awake. He had color in his face, and he focused on me. His eyes followed me as I moved past his bed and to the chair beside him. I said,

"Good morning. You look better today. How are you feeling?"

He cleared his throat and softly said, "I am tired. I can't sleep here: it is too noisy."

"I know it is hard to sleep with the oxygen mask whistling; the IV machine signaling when fluid bags need to be replenished; and the monitor beeping when your heart rate, blood pressure, oxygen saturation, respiration, or temperature fall outside the safety range. Try to think of yourself outside of this hospital room, some place pleasant and peaceful to help you sleep."

He lifted his left hand and pointed to his ribs. He set his fingers down lightly on his chest and said, "My chest hurts."

I asked, "You don't remember anything we have been telling you for the past two weeks?"

He blankly stared at me, asking me with his eyes, What have you been telling me?

I explained, again, that he had been going through acute alcohol withdrawal, and on day six, he had had cardiopulmonary arrest. "You died! While the nurses and doctors were working to resuscitate your heart, they broke some of your ribs."

He looked into my eyes as I continued to tell him about the events of the past two weeks. Tears welled up in the corners of his eyes and a wave of sadness brushed across his face. He turned his head away from me as a tear rolled down his cheek. He did not say anything. He did not say he was sorry or that he wished he had stopped drinking. But the expression on his face was that of remorse; he knew that he was destroying his life—committing a slow suicide.

The intensivist entered the room and greeted us. "How are you today?" he cheerfully asked Val.

Val stared. No response.

The doctor continued, asking the first of two questions the doctors always addressed at the beginning of their patient visits: "Can you tell me where you are?"

Val replied, "I am in the hospital."

"Good," said the intensivist. "And can you tell me your birthday?"

"December 19, 1961," Val said with a heavy sigh. He was irritated that the doctors asked the same two questions each time they visited him. He could always answer those two questions, but he did not remember anything that had happened during the past two weeks.

The intensivist confirmed that Val's blood pressure and oxygen readings were improving, though he would continue to need the oxygen mask. He said, "Val, we would like to perform a coronary angiogram. The purpose of the angiogram is to see if the coronary arteries are narrowed or blocked and to look for abnormalities of heart muscle or heart valves. But we will wait a few days to perform this procedure, once your readings are stable."

The intensivist continued, "Good news. You should be able to eat solid foods starting tomorrow. Real meat and potatoes!" He smiled and said, "Steady as she goes!" He asked if Val had any questions. Val shook his head no. The doctor said, "All right, then. I will see you tomorrow." He said goodbye and left the room.

Val and I looked at each other. I said, "You are improving. It has been a tough two weeks."

He nodded.

I knew he was more aware. He had stopped pointing to his vitals on the monitor and telling me he was better. He had stopped telling me he wanted to go home. I felt he was past the worst.

CHAPTER 21—STEADY AS SHE GOES

DAY 14. Tim greeted me as I walked into the ICU. "Val had a good night last night. He did not have any hallucinations," he said.

"Oh, thank goodness," I replied with relief. "Will he be able to start eating solid foods today?"

"Yes, we have ordered lunch for him. He should have a protein, a vegetable, and a liquid broth and Jell-O." Tim looked at Val and gave him a big smile. "It will be the best meal you have had in weeks!"

Val offered a faint smile.

Tim continued, "Would you like to sit in the chair today?"

Val nodded.

Tim motioned to Juan as he passed the room. Juan stepped inside, and together, the two men lifted Val to the edge of the bed. Val had lost a tremendous amount of strength, and the two struggled to get Val propped upright and balanced. They worked harmoniously to move the IV lines aside, adjust Val's gown, and then, sliding his legs to the edge of the bed, propping his upper body upright, and with a big push, lift him off the bed and into the chair. Success! Val was sitting comfortably in the chair.

Two hours into my visit, as promised, lunch was delivered at noon—a plate of solid foods consisting of a slice of roast beef, mashed potatoes, and a vegetable mix, and a small bowl of brown broth and a cup of Jell-O. It was too much food for someone who hadn't eaten in two weeks. Val picked at his food, taking a small bite of each item on his plate. Then he ate all the mashed potatoes, leaving the rest to get cold before an orderly took the plate away.

We spent the rest of my visit playing *Words with Friends* on our phones. It took a few hours to play three words, but it was an indication that his cognitive skills were improving. He would easily lose concentration and his mind wandered, yet it was the most alert I had seen him, except for his uncanny lucidity when he had awoken from his cardiopulmonary arrest and induced paralysis. I had worried about permanent brain damage the cardiologist had alluded to in previous days but was now somewhat hopeful he would regain his ability to think and remember.

Val was still sitting in his chair when I was ready to leave the hospital. I leaned over him and put my hand on his forehead. I told him I would be back tomorrow and wished him a good night's sleep. He didn't ask me to take him home. He just lifted a weak arm and put his hand on my arm. I took his hand and held it for a moment. Then I said goodbye and turned away.

CHAPTER 22—THE BED IS TOO SOFT

DAY 15. I worked that morning until noon. I heated up a frozen meal for lunch and then drove to the hospital. I thought, *He had such a good day yesterday. He should be sitting in the big turquoise chair and eating another lunch with solid foods. Maybe we will play* Words with Friends *again or watch a movie together. I want to ask again if he remembers anything about his cardiopulmonary arrest or withdrawals. Maybe now that he is more cognizant, he might have some memory. It should be a good day.*

I pulled into the hospital parking lot during the lunch hour, driving around a few lanes before finding a parking stall. The hospital was busy with lunchtime visitors. I made my way past the reception desk and to the hallway of elevators. I took the elevator to the third floor and walked up to the Queen's Guard, but before I could reach for the red button, the big doors slowly opened; Juan, inside the ICU, had seen me on the camera and had opened the doors. Humming, I walked through the doorway and down the hall to room 442.

The room was a flurry of activity. Val was frantically talking to Paul and trying to explain something to him. Val was still wearing the oxygen mask and his voice was faint. Paul was struggling to understand what Val was telling him. I walked over to Val's left side, put my ear to his mouth, and listened to him.

Val raised his right hand and moved it around in a circular motion as he said, "My back, my back."

"Does your back hurt?" I asked.

"Yes," he said, pointing to his right side just above the hip bone.

I told Paul about Val's previous back injuries and that he had lower

157

back pain.

Paul said, "The mattress may be too soft; it is not a thick, support-ive mattress, as it is designed to be moved easily. We have a mattress that has an air pump, and we can use the pump to firm the mattress. It is in the storage closet."

"I think that would help give his lower back more support," I said.

"I will find Juan, and we can bring the air pump mattress and swap it with the soft mattress."

Paul looked at Val. "We are going to take care of you, my friend. We will get you a different mattress," he said before he turned and left the room.

"Thank you," Val replied.

Five minutes later, Paul and Juan returned with the mattress. Paul looked at Val and said, "First, we need to put you in the chair." Then the two men worked together to lift Val to the edge of the bed. When they lifted his upper body, he yelped in pain. Val had never cried out in pain like that with previous back pain. I thought, *His compressed disc must be extremely agitated from lying on a soft mattress for too long. I hope it doesn't cause so much pain it prevents him from physical rehabilitation when he is released from the ICU.*

Paul and Juan were able to lift Val into the chair. As the two men worked quickly to exchange the bedding and mattress, Val continued to whimper and exhibit excruciating pain. When Paul and Juan were finished, they lifted Val from the chair, and he cried out again. His pain had escalated. They placed Val back in bed and tucked pillows around his sides. Val relaxed and stopped whimpering.

Paul asked, "Is the mattress firmer, and does your back feel better?"

Val nodded and then closed his eyes. I decided he should rest. Moving from the bed to the chair and back again had caused him a great deal of pain and exertion. I left the room and would return in the evening.

It was 6:00 p.m., and I was preparing to return to the hospital for a few hours. As I was getting ready to find my purse and car keys, a nurse from the hospital called the home phone. It was Dolly, the first nurse Val had kicked in the head. Dolly said, "Hi, Kym. I am calling to tell you that Val has internal bleeding. The pain we thought was back pain is internal bleeding, and blood is pooling in the peritoneal cavity. This type of bleeding is called a spontaneous retroperitoneal hemorrhage. The cavity is located on his right back side, which is why Val was pointing to that area for his pain."

My throat instantly dried, and I struggled to ask, "Why or from where is he bleeding?"

"We do not know," Dolly replied. "We gave him a unit of blood, and we will monitor his hemoglobin levels. We may have to give him more blood, but for now, it is wait and monitor."

"What happens next if you need to continue giving him blood?"

"We will likely perform an angiogram to locate the source of bleeding."

"Will you perform surgery?"

"Val's doctor will discuss the angiogram and possible surgery with you if that is what the doctor orders. Meanwhile, I think it is best if you stay home this evening. Val needs rest, and we are closely monitoring him."

I thanked Dolly and hung up the phone. I sat in the living room and stared at the black television screen. It wasn't on. I wasn't on. I was numb.

CHAPTER 23—SCHEDULING
A TRANSFER

DAY 16. It was 9:00 a.m. when the home phone rang—Dolly was calling with an update. She said, "Val was given another unit of blood last night. We reversed the blood thinners that were given to him early in his stay in hopes that it would stop the bleeding. The bleeding seemed to stop briefly, but not permanently. We gave him another unit of blood this morning. He is slowly leaking blood."

She continued in a soft-spoken voice, "Last night we gave him a sleep aid to help him sleep, and it had the opposite effect. He became confused and started having the same symptoms he displayed earlier during alcohol withdrawal. He is ranting about being released, and he believes the nurses were hurting him when they put him to bed. He is imagining they were pushing him into his bed and hitting him. He now pulls back from all of us as though he is afraid of being hit."

I slumped in the chair and sullenly asked, "Why would it have an opposite effect, and why after two weeks?"

"It happens sometimes. His confusion is escalating." Dolly hesitated for a moment, then continued, "The doctor is going to recommend transferring him to Northwest hospital. They have a top-notch surgical heart team, and they are better equipped to perform angiograms."

"When will they transfer him?"

"Later this afternoon. The doctor has notified Northwest hospital, and they will transfer him when a room in the ICU is available. The doctor will call you for your approval to make the transfer."

"Should I wait to visit him until he is transferred?"

"It would probably be best. The staff will prepare him for a mobile transfer in an ambulance, and then he will be situated in an ICU room. Remember, the doctor will be calling soon."

I thanked Dolly and hung up the phone. I sat slouching in the chair for several minutes. I thought, *He is bleeding internally, confused, and not recovering. How is he going to survive an angiogram, and what will happen if he needs surgery? He isn't strong enough for surgery.*

A few minutes later the doctor called. He confirmed everything Dolly had explained to me and recommended transferring Val to Northwest hospital. He asked for my permission to transfer him that afternoon to Northwest hospital and I gave it to him. I thanked him for his help and we said goodbye. I stood up and walked outside to sit and gaze at the mountains. I was numb and my thoughts were jumbled. I called my aunt to share the news of Val's condition and to have her comfort me.

Aunt Jody and I talked for twenty minutes. She asked, again, if she could fly down from Washington and stay with me. I told her I appreciated her support but was so tired and numb. I didn't have the energy to share time with anyone. She grudgingly agreed, and we said goodbye.

Still sitting on the patio, I tapped on my cellphone, entered the password, and said, "Okay, Google. What is spontaneous retroperitoneal hemorrhage?" Google displayed the answer: It is a rare clinical entity; signs and symptoms include pain, hematuria, and shock. Spontaneous retroperitoneal hemorrhage can be caused by tumors, such as renal cell carcinoma and angiomyolipoma, polyarteritis nodosa, and nephritis.

I closed the Google screen and set the phone down on the patio table. I thought, *Tomorrow must be a better day for Val—there is no other option.*

CHAPTER 24—ON HOLD

DAY 17. I went to Northwest hospital. I went earlier than usual since I had not visited yesterday and I wanted Val to know I was there for him. I walked into the ICU. I had not been to Northwest hospital before, and it is much older than Oro Valley Hospital. The ICU is tucked away in the center of the building and is very cramped, dark, and smaller than Oro Valley's ICU. I could easily see into other rooms as I made my way to the end of the hallway to Val's room. There was little privacy.

As I approached Val's room, the nurse assigned to Val greeted me and introduced himself as Dave. He was very pleasant, but serious. The atmosphere was depressing, emitting a hopeless vibe. I didn't like it, and I knew it would not be good for Val's psyche, especially if he had episodes of anxiety and hallucinations.

Dave informed me that the angiogram surgery was on hold. Val had not required a unit of blood that morning, a good indication that the leaking may be slowing. He had had a CT scan earlier in the morning, and the scan had revealed that the hemorrhage was slightly larger. The surgeon elected to wait in hopes that the arterial bleeding into the retroperitoneal space would stop on its own.

Before Val had been transferred to Northwest hospital, Dolly had packed up the personal photographs and other personal items from Oro Valley Hospital so they would be in Val's new room. She also suggested I take a favorite robe or pillow because she thought it might give him some comfort to have more items that reminded him of home. She said being in an ICU for so long, coupled with his anxiety, could cause his mind to go a little wacky. I took her advice and took a new set of

163

pictures of our dogs, Lady and Brandy, and a soft robe. I placed the frames on a small table next to the visitor's recliner. I then pulled the robe from my flower-print canvas bag and asked Val if he would like it over his shoulders. He motioned to place it next to him. He must have been warm because he had kicked his sheet off himself and was lying on the bed with his gown pulled halfway up, exposing his genitals. I pulled his gown down and then tucked the robe alongside his pillow. I pointed to the pictures, but he didn't turn to look at them. He just stared at me and then out the door to the nurses' station.

I sat next to him for an hour. I noticed his toenails were ridiculously long, and I asked him if I could trim them. He briefly glared at me and then nodded. He didn't care, but it gave me something to do, and they really were disgusting. I clipped each toenail and then rubbed his feet for him; they felt so cold. I pulled the bed sheet over his body and placed the soft robe over his lower legs and feet.

A nurse arrived to take a blood draw to test his hemoglobin level—a test being performed every six hours. As she was preparing to take blood, I looked at the monitor for his vitals. Suddenly, his blood pressure rocketed to 180 and then fell back down. It was instantaneous!

Surprised, I asked the nurse, "Did you see that spike?"

She said in a sharp tone, "Yes, it was his AFib."

"That was scary," I said in amazement. "I thought his AFib was under control."

"No, he still has AFib."

The nurse seemed annoyed that I was there. She drew Val's blood and then said, "Perhaps you should take a break. Go home for a while."

Taken aback by her attitude, I didn't question her and decided to leave. I gently squeezed Val's hand and said I would be back later in the evening. I didn't return.

Chapter 25—Lady

DAY 18. It was Saturday and the last day of September. Val would be starting a new month tomorrow and was still in an ICU. I thought, *How much longer is he going to stay in an ICU? And why has he stopped asking me to take him home? At least he isn't hallucinating—or if he is, he isn't telling me about his visions. I don't know if he is getting better or worse. For lack of a medical term, he seems stuck in one place, not regressing or improving.*

I arrived at the hospital after lunch and stayed the entire afternoon. Val was quiet, withdrawn. I watched television and held his hand. He turned his head to the right and looked away from me. Occasionally, he would look back toward me, and then look away again. Toward the end of my stay, he looked at me and gently squeezed my hand. He said, "I am so pooped."

I nodded and said, "Why don't you try to sleep some. It is almost six, and I will go home and have dinner. I'll come back tomorrow after you get a good night's rest."

He turned his head to the right again and closed his eyes. I left and drove home. I walked into the house and gave Brandy a big hug and some belly rubs. I headed toward the kitchen to find something frozen for dinner, and the phone rang. "Hello," I answered.

"Is this Kym?" a male voice asked.

"Yes, it is," I said.

"This is Dave from Northwest hospital. I know you just got home, but Val is very agitated. I was wondering if it would help to have you come back to the hospital and see if your presence will calm him down."

I felt despair and responded, "I make his agitation worse. He will ask me to take him home, and when I tell him I can't, he'll get irritated—angry. Then he'll tell me I don't care and to just leave, leave him there and go home."

"Oh. Do you have any suggestions?"

"I have a few. Try giving him ice cream; he likes it. And maybe try to refocus him on something he can tell you about—maybe point out the pictures of the dogs and ask him about them. He loves his dogs."

"I will try."

"Call me if he doesn't improve and you want me to come back. I will try to help."

Dave and I hung up. I took a deep breath and closed my eyes. I thought, *This is never going to end.*

Later in the evening, I called the ICU and spoke with Dave.

"How is Val?" I asked. "Should I visit again this evening?"

"Val's behavior is still erratic, but his negativity has improved," Dave replied. "Val is talking nonstop about his dogs and how much he misses Lady."

"I am so glad to hear his behavior is better. Lady was our dingo dog; she died last month. She died when I was taking her to the emergency center at the Veterinary Specialty Center of Tucson, and he never saw her again. He cried when I came back home without her."

"I understand."

"Well, then I will not visit this evening and will go to bed early. Good night."

"Good night, Kym."

CHAPTER 26—A NEW MONTH

DAY 19. October 1—a new month. It was 6:30 a.m., and I was pouring a cup of coffee when the home phone rang. I set the coffee pot down, swiftly moved to the phone, and answered, "Hello."

The lead nurse in the ICU asked, "Is this Kym?

"Yes," I replied.

The nurse took a deep breath. "Val is in shock. We have been using an oxygen pump, and we can't sustain his oxygen. When we take the oxygen pump away, he goes into cardiac arrest. You better come to the hospital now."

"All right. I will get dressed and come right now." I hung up and dashed to the bedroom closet. I wasn't processing what the nurse had told me. I was distraught, and I knew I had to hurry to the hospital. I slipped into my pants and was starting to pull on a T-shirt when the phone rang again. I dashed back to the phone and answered, "Hello."

"Is this Kym?"

In an abrupt voice I said, "Yes."

"This is your husband's cardiologist," she said calmly. "Val is in cardiopulmonary arrest, and we have been working hard with the oxygen pump, CPR, and . . ."

I interrupted her to ask, "How long have you been working with him?"

She responded, "Ten to fifteen minutes."

"Stop. Just please stop. He has been through so much; let him go." As I was saying those three simple words, "let him go," I thought, *He has been through so much pain and is miserable. It is time to let him go and be in peace.*

167

"You want us to stop?"

"Yes." I hung up the phone and my heart sank. I didn't feel the energy I had experienced with his first cardiopulmonary arrest. I didn't have an awareness of Val or of the Divine Spirit. The Divine Spirit was not giving him a second chance at life as I had thought. Instead, he had been granted a moment to say goodbye to me and to say he was sorry. I knew he was dead. God showed him grace. God relieved his pain.

I called my neighbor Leigh. "Hello," she said in a sleepy voice as I awoke her on that early Sunday morning.

"It is Kym," I said. "Leigh, can you and Shawn take me to the hospital?"

"What is going on?"

"The hospital just called and told me that Val was in cardiopulmonary arrest, and I told them to stop. I think he has died." My eyes filled with tears.

"Yes, come over now. Shawn and I will take you to the hospital."

I met them in their driveway a few minutes later, and we headed to the hospital. I reenacted my conversation with the cardiologist and that I had told the doctor not to resuscitate him—Val had a living will with a do-not-resuscitate order, and I had made the decision to end his life.

Leigh comforted me and told me I had made the right decision. Val was in pain and miserable. Even if he had been released from the hospital, he would have had a poor quality of life.

I nodded my head in agreement.

We pulled into the hospital parking lot fifteen minutes later. I pushed the button at the ICU doors, and after a long, loud buzz, the doors slowly swung open. Another family passed us as they were leaving the ICU; the woman was crying as the man comforted her with his arm around her shoulders. I was about to cry again.

A nurse greeted us. The nurse knew Leigh and they exchanged pleasantries. Then the nurse turned to me and asked, "Are you Kym?"

"Yes," I said.

She pointed to a room directly ahead and said, "Your husband is in this room."

"Is he dead?" I whispered. I thought, *Why am I asking? I know the answer. But it is imperative that I ask.*

"Yes," she said. "I am so sorry for your loss."

"Thank you."

"Do you want to see him now and collect his belongings?"

I looked at Leigh and again started to cry. I froze. I didn't want to see Val dead. I wanted my last memory of him to be of the day before when he was telling me how pooped he was and then gently closing his eyes. I had seen my mother dead, lying naked on her bed, waiting for the paramedics to take her away—and that is the image I replay when I think of her. I didn't want to do the same with Val. I looked at Leigh and asked, "Do I have to go in?"

She reached her hand out to hold mine and said, "No, you don't have to go."

"I will go in," Shawn said. He turned and walked to the room and then slipped behind the closed curtain.

I stared at the curtain. My feet wanted to take me to Val' s room, but I didn't move. I wanted to tell him goodbye, but I didn't move my feet. I couldn't walk forward and past the curtain.

The nurse stayed with me and Leigh. She gave me some pamphlets for funeral homes and the next steps to take after death.

A few minutes later, Shawn moved the curtain open with his right hand while his left hand held a bag. He had gathered the pictures, blanket, phone, wedding ring, and cane—Val's belongings. He slowly walked up to us and gave me a weak smile. "He is still intubated," he said. "You probably don't want to see him that way."

I nodded in agreement, and the three of us turned and slowly walked toward the exit. No one said goodbye. No doctors spoke to me. No one offered suggestions for dealing with bereavement. We just slowly left the hospital and left Val behind. Gone forever.

CHAPTER 27—RENEWAL

The days following Val's death were long and lonely—empty! I felt as though a thick fog blanketed me and I couldn't remove the blanket. My thoughts and movements felt slow. I replayed the scenes from the three weeks in the ICU repeatedly in my mind. Tears often welled in my eyes, teetering on the edges, then spilling over and down my cheeks. I was torn between being alone and losing my husband and being thankful he was no longer suffering from the constant pain from peripheral neuropathy and alcoholism.

I pictured him waking up each morning and walking with his awkward, wide gait, uneasy with his balance, to the kitchen for a cup of coffee. Then moving unsteadily to the living room couch to sit down, where he would remain for the rest of the day and into the evening, until he was ready to start the whole process over again. He would sit on the couch and set his coffee mug down on the small round glass table. Not more than ten minutes would pass, and he would be crying. The pain in his legs was merciless and started almost immediately after he stood up from his bed.

He would pray every morning before he rose that when his feet touched the floor, his legs would not start to have the burning, shooting pain he felt all day until he had his first drink of whiskey. As his tears formed wet spots on his white T-shirt, the only shirts he wore, he would look at me with his lost, wet eyes and ask why this was happening to him. Then he would tell me he no longer wanted to be here, on earth—alive. I would listen and show him compassion, but I wouldn't offer an explanation—what was the point; he had made his choice to continue to drink. He was stuck.

For a month, I could not shake those images from my mind. I cried every day. And every night. Each morning after showering, I would go into the closet and put my arms around his white T-shirts still hanging together, never to be worn again. I would nestle my face into the T-shirts and inhale deeply. The shirts smelled like Val, and for a moment, I felt connected to him. I felt a loss. I felt grief. And yes, sometimes I felt relief. I was free from my life with an alcoholic. I was free to Heal.

My neighbors, Shawn and Leigh, were supportive and helped me through my grieving. They invited me to dinner or to the local brewery to watch Sunday Night Football and have sliders and a beer. I talked and enjoyed their company, but I still felt distant and struggled to socialize. I often felt like Charlie Brown when the teacher, Miss Othmar, was talking to the kids: "Wah wah, woh wah."

About a week after Val died, Michael, a previous co-worker from before I began my consulting practice, sent me flowers and a sympathy card. This was not your typical fifty-dollar bouquet of flowers. The flowers arrived in a large basket that was full of large sunflowers, peach and orange roses, and red and orange carnations. Leigh stopped over to visit just after the flowers arrived. I pointed out to her the lovely flowers from Michael. She smiled and told me how pretty they were and that he must care about me. I did not catch on, but she was thinking, *Wow, that is an expensive basket of flowers, and that man is going to keep in touch with Kym.*

A few weeks later, Leigh and I went to lunch, and I casually mentioned Michael. She said, "He is going to marry you someday." I smiled and didn't have much of a response. Surprised by her awareness of my fondness for Michael, and feeling a little guilty that Val had died less than a month ago, I realized Michael was slowly drifting into my thoughts. A few days later, Michael was roaming my thoughts every day. I reminded myself about how well we had worked together so many years ago and how I had admired his work ethic and his loyalty to friends and family. I admitted to myself that he had made my heart light up when he entered a room. Thirty years had passed since I had first met Michael, and he still made me feel like a schoolgirl with a crush. The thought made me laugh.

I continued to think about Michael more and more. I was a widow and he was soon to be divorced. Within five weeks, we would both be single. For thirty years, one or both of us had been committed to other people. My desire to reach out and tell him that I cared for him grew stronger. I knew I had to tell him, but how? I had to be subtle. After all, I had just lost my husband, and he was losing his wife and family. But I feared that if I did not take a chance and tell him he made my heart glow, then I might lose the opportunity forever. I had kept my feelings buried for thirty years, and I never thought I would have a chance to be with the man I respected, admired, and, yes, loved.

A travel catalog was sitting on my kitchen counter. I thought I would write him a letter, explaining how my husband, years ago, had become immersed in alcoholism, self-pity, and pain. I would send him the travel catalog and ask him to travel with me. It was the perfect plan to begin my love affair with him.

A few months earlier, when he and I had been discussing his divorce, he had commented, "I should have married you."

I replied, "You should have."

He said, "Yeah, but you were always with Val. If we are both single when we are sixty, let's travel the world together."

And I replied, "You've got a deal."

I wrote the one-page letter and asked him to travel with me. I put Post-it Notes on some of the pages with hikes of interest, enclosed the letter and catalog in a plain manila envelope, sealed it, and mailed it to Michael, who lived in the Midwest. For the next few days, I was nervous. I wondered if he would reject my request. I wondered if he liked me or ever thought about me the way I had thought about him for the past thirty years. Sure, we always flirted with one another, but that doesn't always mean that two people want to spend time together and grow a relationship—they just have a natural chemistry.

About a week passed, and on Friday he called me. Of course I missed the call. Darn! I emailed him at work, told him I was in the office, and asked him to please call back. He did. He told me he had received the catalog and would love to take a trip with me. He, of course, teased me about earmarking the pages for hikes that interested me, but that was how we usually interacted, open and carefree with one another. He was complimentary and told me I was attractive, smart, and fun and that he would love to travel with me.

Not hesitating to show my excitement, I asked him to pick a trip and we could plan something for the next year. I knew I made him happy that a woman, especially one he had known for so many years, was interested in his company. It was the boost he needed after months of negotiating a divorce. And his elated response made me happy. I too needed someone to be interested in being with me. I had become a caretaker over the last several years—no, not years but decades—and I was yearning for a friendship and partnership. I was yearning to be wanted, not needed. To love and be loved. To enjoy and be enjoyed.

A month later, we planned our first trip, but it wasn't until the following October. Through the holidays, we occasionally exchanged texts—sharing pleasantries and catching up on the holidays' festivities. During January, Michael was busy working on a merger and acquisition of the company that employed him. On January 25, a final, agreed-upon contract to sell the company had been signed by both buyer and seller, and I was anxious to call him and congratulate him. We missed each other's calls for a few days until, finally, we connected on a Sunday afternoon. He was shopping with his daughter and was waiting in the mall when he returned my call and I answered. I told him I was calling to congratulate him about the sale. What I was really calling for was to tell him I wanted to see him and soon, much sooner than next October. While he sat at the mall and talked with me, we made small talk for a few minutes, and then he suggested visiting his brother in Oregon to celebrate the sale of the company and that he would stop and celebrate with me in Tucson. He continued to talk about his brother, telling me what he was like and what he did for a living. He then said, "He is single; I could introduce you to him."

I said, "No." I thought, *Are you dense? How much hinting and flirting do you need to realize I want to be with you, to touch you, to hold you, to run my fingers through your thick gray hair?* Apparently, I had to be blunt. I said, "Michael, I need to tell you how I feel about you."

He replied, "How do you feel about me?"

I proceeded to tell him about one evening when we were both in our twenties and traveling in St. Louis. We were on a large audit, and we stayed for two weeks without going back home for the weekend. We swam in the hotel pool, and we both enjoyed swimming up to one another, pulling each other underwater, and flirting. I was wearing a sexy black bikini, and I could tell he was watching me—looking at my body. We went to dinner that evening and, as usual, had a nice meal and a few drinks. We were back at the hotel by 9:00 that evening. I went to my room and sat for a few moments in the dark, contemplating my next move.

I told him how, that night in St. Louis, I sat on the side of the bed for a few minutes before turning on the lamp and picking up the phone, nervously dialing his hotel room. I was nervous and almost hung up. It rang once, then twice, and then three times. After the sixth ring, I hung up the phone. I had called to ask him to come to my room—to be with me. It never happened.

I was attracted to Michael because he was fun, career-oriented, and happy. But I was living with Val, and I was in a committed relationship. That night in the hotel was the only time I attempted to be with another man. I knew back then, in St. Louis, before I married Val, that Val was not the best choice for a life-long partner.

After thirty years, I was finally telling Michael that I wanted him. I did not need him. I had no demands of him. I simply wanted him; I wanted his body and soul.

My confession did not seem to surprise him, and he asked, "Where was I when you called my room? Why didn't I answer the phone?"

"I have no idea—perhaps asleep," I replied.

I knew he felt something for me too. He just hadn't explored the idea; he hadn't let our flirtation and admiration for one another surface.

He jumped in with both feet and suggested, "We can meet before our planned October trip. Where should we go? How will I introduce you to my children? How do you feel about children? We will have to take it slow, especially for my children. They have been through a rough divorce, and my ex-wife has a new boyfriend."

"I like large families, and yes, we will take it slow. Let's take our first trip and see what happens."

He agreed, and we planned our first date in Las Vegas. Viva Las Vegas, baby! In two weeks, February 16, we were going to share a hotel room and discover each other. We had never kissed, so I tried to imagine our first kiss.

A few days passed and we yearned to see one another. We talked and shared texts. We became more and more engrossed in flirting and teasing one another, opening up and sharing our desires. He texted that he longed to feel my body next to his. Then, shortly after, he said, "I really want to feel you against me. I want to learn how to make your body quiver. I want to know what you sound like when you orgasm." Within a few days of texting, we had lost sight of the word "SLOW." But our conversations were not just about body chemistry. We both seemed to miss each other, even though we had never dated. We both wanted a deeper relationship.

The night before our trip to Las Vegas, Michael called and said, "I can't wait to see you. I am divorced and damaged, but the idea of starting something with you excites me. I would not be starting a relationship with anyone else but you. We have a foundation of friendship, loyalty, and trust. I am looking for the love story—the "happily ever after" story. I want you to know me better than anyone has ever known me, and I want to know you the same way. I want your body and soul. Shooting for less is not an option for me."

"I want the same thing. This is important for both of us."

"Good. I am very excited."

"So am I."

It was travel day! We had flirted, teased, and talked about having a true love story, and we were just beginning our first date. We were not to be disappointed. We made each other feel alive, feel loved! It was the most exhilarating three days of sensuality, entertainment, culinary delights, more sensuality, embracement, and more love than I had experienced in an exceedingly long time. I could write a book about those three days, and maybe someday I will.

But our timing was wrong, or maybe it was the exact timing for both of us to feel ignited and alive.

I moved to his home state, and the first three months were glorious. His children were out of school for the summer, and while they were staying with their mom, Michael and I could spend quality time together. But we both brought issues from our previous marriages. And as noted in Melody Beattie's *Codependent No More*, our communication reeked of repressed feelings, repressed thoughts, ulterior motives, and anger (toward our spouses). And I, having codependency characteristics, started my old behavior patterns of wanting to help him with his children, make family dinners, and organize his home. He had told me he wanted to move slowly, especially with his children. And as a codependent caregiver and helper, I didn't listen to what he was saying, or perhaps what he was not saying. He was not saying he wanted me to move into his home anytime soon. He was not saying he wanted or needed my help to run his household. I wanted so badly to be part of his life; I simply did not listen.

And he wasn't any better at communicating. Instead of discussing a timeline for us to be a "family," he would avoid the subject and not include me in family gatherings—birthday parties, Thanksgiving, or decorating the Christmas tree. I didn't even meet the children for five months after having relocated to his home state. And when I was finally introduced to the children, ranging in ages ten to eighteen, and invited to the home, he didn't want me organizing or changing anything inside the home. I suggested I was a team player and wanted to help, and his response was, "You are a team player, even when you are the only one on the team." He was sarcastic, and he demonstrated that he could not clearly articulate his feelings and needs.

It was obvious we were not on the same page in our relationship. And it was obvious he didn't want me in his children's lives, or perhaps his, for that matter.

A year later, soon after Christmas, we parted as the devoted friends we had always been, no hard feelings or regrets.

CHAPTER 28—TIME TO PLAN

It had been a year and a half since Val's death. I had lost, grieved, awakened, learned, forgiven, loved again, lost again, and found my inner strengths and passions—my passions for life, friendships, companionship, and everything else that makes us feel alive.

I had had a year and a half to accept my past life with Val, to forgive him, to forgive myself, to move forward.

I planned a return visit to Jackson, Wyoming—our favorite place the two of us shared for ten years. We built our first architect-designed home in Jackson on a butte in between Jackson and Wilson in a subdivision called Bar Y. The home was perched on five acres and had expansive views of the mountains to the east, south, and west. Deer, elk, and moose crisscrossed the yard in the winter, and the chipmunks chased each other around the circular stone flower bed on the warm summer days. That was undeniably Val's favorite residence. It was there he wanted to have his ashes spread upon his death.

It was June, and I was busy packing for my drive from the desert valley floor in Tucson to the lush green mountains in Jackson. I had my clothes, my favorite daypacks and hiking gear, the dog's pillow, and her food and treats all packed and lined up in the hallway leading to the garage. It was time to pack the ashes. It seemed respectful to pack the ashes last, and I had four packages to pack. I was taking the ashes of three of our dogs, Karo, BJ and Lady, as well as Val's ashes. Karo was our first dog. We adopted her from a Seattle animal shelter when she was eight weeks old. She was a sassy little German shepherd mix. BJ came into our lives a year after Karo. He had failed the Canine Companion for Independence program, and we were elated to have him in our forever home. Lady was adopted in Jackson along with her kennel mate, Brandy. The two were adopted shortly after Karo and BJ had died. Lady was a docile, sweet, and loving pharaoh hound mix, and Brandy was a buddy for life beagle-boxer mix.

The dogs' ashes rested in beautiful handmade blue-green and burgundy clay vases. I removed the vases from the china cabinet where they had protected Karo's and BJ's ashes for the past decade and Lady's ashes for the last year and a half.

I carried the vases to the kitchen counter next to the window overlooking the front porch and western sky. I gently removed the lids of each vase and placed them on the kitchen counter. The tallest vase held BJ's ashes. He had been a plump golden retriever, and his ashes required the larger vase. The sympathy card on the top of the pile caught my eye. It was a picture of a rainbow, and all the colors were crisp and bright as though it had been printed yesterday. I picked up the card and started to read, "By the edge of a wood, at the foot of a hill, is a lush, green meadow where time stands still. Where the friends of man and woman do run when their time on earth is done. For here, between this world and the next, is the place where beloved dogs find rest. . . ." I continued, smiling as visions of young versions of the dogs frolicked through the field in my mind.

I removed BJ's collar, dog tag, and sympathy cards and placed them next to the vase lid. I then lightly twisted and slowly tugged on the plastic bag holding his ashes. The bag was snug. I gently pried it free from its slumbering place and set it in a small black travel bag. I then moved to the vase containing Karo's belongings and ashes and performed the same careful procedure of removing her contents. Her collar had a pungent odor that reminded me of when she would roll in elk poop or anything dead and decaying. Memories of our long hikes in the mountains brought a joyful grin to my face. I placed her bag of ashes in the travel bag alongside BJ's ashes. Finally, I opened Lady's urn. A white urn protected her ashes and a plaster print of her paw, a forever keepsake. I placed her bag of ashes in the travel bag. All three dogs had had the joy of living at the house in Bar Y. They surely would be pleased to return to Bar Y for their journey-after-life celebration.

Then it was time to get Val's ashes. I walked back to the china cabinet and picked up the beautifully polished wooden box that guarded

Val's ashes. Along with his ashes, I had placed other treasures: his wedding ring, the Swiss watch I had purchased on a hiking trip with my aunt in Switzerland, his driver's license, pictures of him, his death certificate, and all the sympathy cards I had received upon his death.

I placed the box on the kitchen counter beside the empty pottery vases. I glided my hand across the smooth, shiny top. I placed both hands on the sides of the box and left them there for a few minutes to feel the box and visualize the contents. I lifted the box's lid to see the cards draped over the packaged ashes. I read each card, and then read them again. I had forgotten the number of cards and the kind thoughts people had shared. I reflected on the warmheartedness of friends and family as I set the cards on the counter.

I touched the soft, tan velvet bag that contained another box with Val's ashes. I placed my hands around the velvet bag, and a sudden rush of warmth filled my chest, flowing from the center of my body outward, moving to my arms and out my fingertips. My entire upper body was warm and tingling as I felt comfort and joy. It felt as though Val was sharing the moment with me. It was one moment he could tell me he was there, and I would know it was him because I was holding his remains. The energetic exchange in the ICU was happening again—an instantaneous understanding and communication, an undeniable presence. I sensed his appreciation and love and an undeniable connection that continued in the afterlife. He shared that he was pleased I was taking his remains to Jackson—his final resting place on earth. And without words, I expressed my happiness for him, comforted by the thought that he was in a blissful place, free of pain and sadness. I knew he was watching over me, leaving gifts, tiny clues, to take a health-giving, healing PATH forward, giving me purpose, joy, and love.

I stood in the kitchen with my hands on the velvet bag. The warmth flooded me for a minute, maybe longer, leaving me relaxed and content. Val's spirit was touching my hands and my spirit, guiding me to lift the velvet-covered box of ashes out of the wooden box. As I lifted the box out, the warmth slowly receded, but a presence remained. I carefully placed the velvet-covered box in the travel bag. I had four spirits ready to transport to Jackson—to release the ashes in a place of unspoiled beauty, a place where all four would rejoice.

CHAPTER 29—SHIFTING WINDS

It was late June when I arrived in Jackson. My friend Lori and I made plans to have the memorial the following week. Two evenings before the memorial, as I drifted toward sleep, a slight energy moved within me and stirred an image. The image was in color and was a picture with two words across the top. In the picture stood a lean, young man with medium-length brownish hair wearing a dark blue, long-sleeved, collared cotton shirt and blue jeans. His back was turned, standing on a hillside, peering miles ahead to an open field where the sun shone. His left arm was lifted halfway up as though he was reaching for the sunlight dancing in the tall grasses. Billowy, dark, bluish-gray clouds swirled above, but in the far-off distance, they were shifting to the sides as though to make room for the sunlight to envelop the field.

Eyes closed, I focused on the two words. The letters were blurry, but I could make out the words "Shifting Winds." Surprised, I thought, *This is the title to my book about living with an alcoholic, and a chapter title.* Our journey through life, like the sea, will ebb and flow and, like the shifting winds, will change course.

The next day, one day before the memorial, Brandy and I sat outside my Jackson condo on the deck. It was a wonderfully warm day, and I enjoyed sitting, feeling the sunshine's warmth, and looking out to Munger Mountain. I had in my hand a book Lori had given me entitled *Earth Prayers from Around the World: 365 Prayers, Poems, and Invocations for Honoring the Earth.* I opened the book and started looking for some meaningful poems or quotes to read at Val's memorial. I flipped through the pages, randomly stopping to read a prayer or poem, then flipped back and forth and stopped to read another one.

I read about fifteen prayers and poems until I read one that touched my soul: one that made me feel tenderness and love, one that made me smile and cry. This was the poem I was going to read at the memorial. The poem, with no title, was by Joyce Fossen. I read it aloud several times, practicing the pauses:

> *Do not stand at my grave and weep.*
> *I am not there. I do not sleep.*
>
> *I am a thousand winds that blow.*
> *I am the diamond glint on snow.*
>
> *I am the sunlight on ripened grain.*
> *I am the gentle autumn rain.*
>
> *When you wake in the morning hush*
> *I am the swift, uplifting rush*
> *of quiet birds in circling flight.*
> *I am the soft starlight at night.*
>
> *Do not stand at my grave and weep.*
> *I am not there. I do not sleep.*[15]

The perfect poem! I walked from the patio to the kitchen, setting the book on the kitchen island. It was time to gather the items for the memorial and put them also on the kitchen island. I fetched the small black travel bag I had packed with the ashes I brought from Tucson. I hadn't moved or opened the bag since unpacking it from the car and storing it in the guest room. I set the bag on the kitchen island and put my hands on top of it, then gently pressed down. Energy coursed through my core and I felt a presence. I closed my eyes: the energy flowed through my body, running down my arms and into each finger, springing upward into my throat and head. I stood in the kitchen with my eyes closed and saw more color images, clearer than before. The first image was of BJ, my goofy, happy-go-lucky golden retriever. He was up on his hind legs and bobbing up and down as though looking for a biscuit—begging as usual. He was wagging his tail and was a

15. Roberts and Amidon, *Earth Prayers*, 30.

much thinner BJ than when he had died.

An observation I have made with all my images—dogs and people all appeared middle-aged. The faces were smooth with no wrinkles or blemishes, their bodies fit and lean. I gave thought to the faces because, until the previous day, my images had been only of the shoulders and heads, and only black and white.

The second image was of Val. He was walking away, his body half turned toward me. Then he stopped, turned fully toward me, and smiled. Without speaking, he communicated that he was here, looking over me. He was free of earthly ills and pain. He turned again and slowly walked away, toward a valley with low-lying hills. He was wearing a long-sleeved, collared blue shirt and blue jeans. As I watched his image move away, I knew he had been the person in my drifting sleep the previous night; and I knew he was at peace.

I set the book of poems and the scissors, for cutting open the bags of ashes, inside the travel bag—I was ready for the memorial.

The next day, Friday, July 12, was a beautiful, sunny day. White clouds drifted past, heading toward the Teton mountain range. Lori was driving me to the memorial site, our previous Bar Y home. Lori had designed additions to the house for the current owners, and she had asked permission to spread Val's ashes. They had agreed, as they were not planning to be at the home until the end of the month.

She picked me up at 11:00 a.m. and we drove to Bar Y. She drove up the winding road and turned into the long driveway that led to the house. We parked and pulled our belongings from the car. I took some pictures of the house and then selected a site for the memorial. I picked the west side of the house where the living room overlooked Teton Pass. We walked through the yard and up the bank of wildflowers, making our way several hundred feet behind the house. I set the black travel bag down and unzipped it. I pulled out Lady's ashes first. I told her to be free and chase the chipmunks as I scooped out handfuls of ashes and tossed them into the light breeze. Next was BJ, and then Karo.

I turned to Lori and explained I was going to read a poem; say a few words about my thirty-nine years with Val; spread his ashes; read a quote from *First15*, a daily devotional app; and then have her lead us in the Lord's Prayer. She agreed to the plan and then turned on my phone's video recorder to capture the moment. I read the poem. It was as touching as the first times I had read it, and I almost cried again. I then told of our married life and said goodbye. I placed my right hand in the plastic bag and scooped a handful of ashes. As I tossed the handful, the breeze caught the ashes and held them in the air, making a blanket of dust before dropping to the ground, covering the wildflowers. I put my hand back into the plastic bag and scooped another handful. I tossed the ashes, only to have the light breeze shift, making another blanket to be placed over a different patch of wildflowers. I repeated the process several times, each time the breeze shifting direction and spreading the ashes over different, unsuspecting wildflowers. As I tossed my last handful, I looked down at my feet to see my shoes covered in a light dusting of ashes. I thought, *Shifting Winds. This chapter title is perfect*!

I continued the memorial and read some excerpts from the *First15* app. I read aloud: "The Holy Spirit gives spiritual gifts to each of us. He *'apportions'* them according to his perfect wisdom. Spiritual gifts are never birthed by man and never given for selfish purposes. The Spirit gives us gifts because he loves us and others. All that he does is in perfect love and is for *'the common good.'* Whether you've been given the gift of wisdom, knowledge, faith, healing, miracles, prophecy, . . . your purpose in the gift is to be the same as the Holy Spirit's: love."[16]

I explained to Lori that my experience with Val in the ICU was one of compassion. Val went to a better place, one without pain and addictions, and I was set free to take a pathway best for me—rebuilding my life and inviting the next houseguests to my home—freedom, joy, laughter, sharing, and love. I had clarity, compassion, and courage for myself.

I continued to read from one of the devotional segments of the *First15* app where it quoted 1 Peter 4:10: "As each has received a gift, use it to serve one another."[17] Lori and I then held hands, and she read the Lord's Prayer. We hugged, said goodbye to the four spirits, and walked back to the car. I was at peace. We were all at peace.

---

16. Denison, "The Gifts of the Holy Spirit."
17. Denison, "The Gifts of the Holy Spirit."

CHAPTER 30—THREE YEARS LATER

As I am typing this chapter, it has been almost three years since the exact date of Val's death. I am still at peace and feel an amazing sense of freedom. I am free to just be me—free to be present in the moment and not worry about the alcoholic. The guesthouse visitors of embarrassment, fear, and anger have been replaced by openness, joy, and peace. My life is amazing!

I have met a kindhearted, thoughtful, funny, and intelligent man, Stephen. As a physician, with additional training in the field of integrative medicine, he has helped me understand the dynamics that can emerge with an alcoholic. Integrative mind-body medicine integrates the best of modern evidence-based medical practices with traditional healing systems, while honoring the multi-dimensionality of the human condition and the mind-body connection.

I have continued my attendance with Al-Anon and have read countless books about alcoholism. But I have never understood how much I changed through Val's stages of alcoholism, and I have never understood how much I contributed to the alcoholic's life. I was stuck in trying to understand Val, not myself.

One day, Stephen and I were on a long drive to New Mexico for a weekend getaway, and I was sharing stories about Val. During the conversation, to capture my full attention, Stephen said, "In some ways, you and Val were a perfect match."

I was shocked. "A perfect match?" I asked.

"Yes."

"How could we be a perfect match? I was responsible and took care of our family needs. I tried to help Val with bettering himself—learning, growing, and expanding his horizons."

"Exactly. You took on most of the responsibilities instead of letting him experience the consequences of his addiction. As is the case for many, the traits you both brought to the dance originated in your formative years. You both had needs and patterns that stemmed from dynamics with your parents and your observations of their respective dynamics, and then ultimately with each other as you ventured out into adulthood."

"Stephen, I don't like hearing that I was destined to be attracted to and marry someone who would become an alcoholic. I should have seen it."

"Try not to use the words 'should have'—you can't change what is done, and it can lead to judgmental, unhealthy thinking. You were young and didn't have the awareness to recognize the behavioral patterns in your relationship or the skills to know how to deal with such behaviors."

"It was a painful and lengthy learning experience—one I pray I will never encounter again!"

We continued to talk during the drive to New Mexico. As we shared stories about our parents, marriages, and families, I occasionally drifted into the thought about my being a perfect match with Val. It made me uncomfortable, and I would have to do a little more soul-searching to understand why I had been attracted to Val and how my traits had promoted and supported his alcoholism and undesirable behaviors. Most definitely, I had tried to fix Val—I had always told myself I was "helping" Val. That is not a good trait in any relationship. I thought about my brief relationship with Michael and my drive to "help" Michael with his children, wanting to make his life easier as he juggled work and being a divorced parent of four children. It wasn't my place to help, and it wasn't a foundation for a lifetime relationship. I had acted as a caregiver, even when my help wasn't requested.

As cited in *Codependent No More*, "The surest way to make ourselves crazy is to get involved in other people's business, and the quickest way to become sane and happy is to tend to our own affairs."[18]

---

18. Beattie, *Codependent No More*, 113.

Chapter 31—To the Family Member

A long chapter in my life is closed, and I continue to reflect, not dwell, on the events of that chapter. The feeling of freedom was almost immediate after Val's death. But I had to earn inner peace through personal reflection. I survived the terrible years of watching my husband slowly commit suicide; I survived the feeling of being used, unloved, and neglected. I rebuilt my life with the loving ears and helping hands of friends and family—learning about my codependent characteristics and what I contributed to the dance. And learning to change my behaviors, although I must continue to work on communication and taking responsibility for my behaviors and choices. I found my inner strength and built upon my optimism and joy of sharing with friends and family. I rekindled my desire to touch, embrace, caress, and deeply love.

On my reflection of events, I see the gifts that have been laid before me:

- Witnessing Val's spirit ascend while his lifeless body was being worked on by nurses and doctors trying to revive him in room 442.
- Learning that the spirit lies within every one of us.
- Val being granted his wish to stay on earth for a period of time so he could hold my hands and sincerely apologize for his demise and the demise of our life together.
- The book *Proof of Heaven,* which opened my mind to the spiritual events in the hospital, to have an awareness of unconditional love.

- Having a brief and passionate relationship with Michael, reopening my heart to love and vulnerability.
- Meeting Stephen, who helped me understand my codependency in childhood and how underlying dynamics impacted my journey with Val.
- Having the courage and desire to author this book and share my story—to change my life and perhaps yours. By reading this book, it is my hope you will be inspired to choose a different life PATH, which would be yet another gift.

I will feel loss again. I will feel hurt again. But the freedom, happiness, and love I embrace will far outweigh those sad moments in life. Without love, humans have little purpose. The ultimate message is simple—love yourself and others. But remember, feel your own feelings first, without self-judgment, gently caring for and loving yourself. Rescuing or caretaking others is not always an act of love, especially when one's needs are denied or undermined.

I think about how many of you, my readers, women and men, are still in those relationships, allowing yourselves to be defined and controlled by the addict in your family. I stated in the Introduction, "As the alcoholic moves through the stages of alcoholism, you, the family member, move through phases on the PATH (figure 1), which, interestingly, often parallel the stages of alcoholism."

Behavior of the addict's family often mirrors the addict's behaviors, but with a focus on the addict instead of an object or thing. These behaviors may include denial, obsession with the addict, compulsion to control the addict, tolerance, shame, isolation, unkindness, and emotional and physical illness. And the family members play roles that enliven these behaviors.

Which family roles are you playing? Examples of roles include victim, chief enabler, family hero, scapegoat, mascot, and lost child. It is time the family member stops playing unhealthy family roles and ends unhealthy helping, which takes away the opportunity for the person struggling with substance use to feel the full impact of their choices.

I spent a considerable amount of time asking "why" and "what" about the addict in my life. I realized there was a need to know the answers—although I could not change Val's life journey, and it was not my responsibility to change it for him. Knowing why his behavior changed over the years helped me understand the stages of alcoholism and helped me understand the things I could change, accept the things I could not change, and know the difference between the two. I could not change Val's life journey; I can, however, change my journey and my PATH. I can Heal.

Understanding the experiences in my life, especially in my formative years, gave clarity to why I was attracted to an addict. Seeing myself and learning about patterns and personality traits helps me control behavioral patterns and choices and avoid repeating harmful patterns. I brought about change. Unfortunately, my husband couldn't be part of my new equation for change, but I could still reinforce healthy, positive recovery behaviors for myself.

It is time for you, the family member, to slow down the emotional roller coaster of life with an addict or get off the roller coaster. It is time to detach from this life you have been living. Are you ready to make a change in your PATH? A new goal for each family member of an alcoholic is allowing the addict to feel the consequences of their substance abuse (physical and behavioral) while positively reinforcing the healthy behaviors that will bring about change.

Do you remember that you can't change, control, or cure alcoholism? Do your actions reflect that understanding? Do you know what makes you happy and inspires you to put both feet on the floor every morning and stand up out of bed? Embrace that motivation to put one foot forward every day and take hold of the present—move your feet forward, taking small steps, then giant steps—even if those steps mean detaching and sometimes leaving someone else behind. Choose what YOU want and make it happen. Set goals. Learn to communicate your feelings and set boundaries—say what you mean and mean what you say. Make healthy choices. Connect with others for support, especially if you are depressed, can't seem to solve your own problems, or have been the victim of psychological, emotional, physical, or sexual abuse.

Connecting is crucial. Reach out to those who can help you—a caring friend, addiction treatment centers that include support programs for families, nonprofit organizations, a church, a counselor, local community safety network organizations that offer shelter and help plot safety plans, or a national network of people including the Office on Violence Against Women (OVW) and the National Domestic Violence Hotline. Someone is out there to help you take those small steps forward that eventually become giant steps forward. Remember first, connect to yourself, then you can connect to others in a healthier way. As my friend Stephen often reminds me, you must know your own note before knowing the note of others. And my favorite Al-Anon slogan: let it begin with me.

Finding your PATH will bring you peace and freedom.

CHAPTER 32—TO VAL AND THE ADDICT

If you can hear me in heaven, it may surprise you to know I miss the man I knew in his twenties and thirties. I miss the man who would take long walks with me on the beaches with our dogs, the man who would grocery shop with me and help prepare meals, the man who would help with housework and yard work on the weekends, and the man who would go to bed with me and hold me until I fell asleep. I miss my best friend. But I am free from your addiction. I am happy. And I know you are at peace.

Unfortunately, I know if you had survived your stay in the ICU, you would not have stopped drinking and we would not be together. If we could go back in time, could you have changed the chain of events that led to your addiction to alcohol and progressive decline? If I had the knowledge I have today about alcoholism and the impact it has on the addict as well as the family member, what would I have done differently? I would have shared with you the stages of alcoholism and the impact it has on physical and emotional behavior—for you and me, the family member. I would have asked you to seek professional help for both your anger issues and your addiction. I would have asked you, my best friend, to be aware of your addictive personality's selfish and mean behavior. I would have set a boundary and asked for a commitment to change.

But sharing my knowledge with you would not have made a difference. Why? Because you were unaware you had a drinking problem. You couldn't admit you were an alcoholic and that you needed help;

you proudly confessed your love for alcohol and never tried to hide your drinking or the bottle of alcohol. Even if deceit had been another layer of your dysfunction, you still would have been in complete denial. Your addictive personality had such a strong grip that you were going to have to experience the bottom—complete despair and unrelenting pain and anguish. I believe I would have had to have the courage to recognize you weren't going to change, and I would have detached from our marriage. And your journey would have ended the same way, in an early death. You believed the alcohol made you feel good and that it dulled your pain. It also filled the void of love in your heart caused by your father's behaviors towards you when you were a child. Val, for you, denial and delusion were your guests in your guesthouse, and they were killers.

To my readers with addiction: That was my husband's journey. But you don't have to follow Val's downward spiral of hopelessness, despair, and fear; never aware of what causes the pain, thus no escape from the pain. You must find your Self—your nonaddictive personality.

You must desire to get off the painful emotional roller coaster of life as an addict. Only you can open your eyes and see that you can go no further living a life of momentary and illusionary feelings of well-being. You can go no further rationalizing your behaviors and saying it isn't your fault and that you aren't to blame. Does that mean you are a bad person? No! Must you be ashamed? No! Does that mean you are unloved? No!

Stop the denial and seek help by connecting with something greater than yourself, something beyond your pain. You will need a recovery program, loving and helpful friends, and when possible, an understanding family. Becoming aware of oneself can be painful. Oh heck—let's be honest, it will be painful. Your years of suffering have triggered addiction, and now you will have to deal with the awareness of your suffering as well as the suffering you have caused others. Learn to resolve the underlying driver of your suffering and find a new PATH forward in renewal, such that when addiction urges emerge, you have a skillset, the power, and the support to experience those urges differently and make better choices.

You can recover, and so can your family members and other loved ones. Remember, addiction is a family disease. It is never too late for a new awareness that you can embrace renewal and reach out to your loved ones and others for help. I wish Val had reached out to me to start the process of finding help. I wish Val hadn't died living a life of denial.

Stop any denial. Only you can find the wisdom and the courage to change. Learn how to free yourself from the chains of addiction and free your loved ones from their suffering due to your addiction. Freedom from hopelessness, despair, fear, and pain is the basis of happiness. Find your PATH to healing and happiness. Set yourself and your loved ones free.

CHAPTER 33—GET HELP

As the reader of this book, you are most likely in a relationship with an addictive person, or you know someone who is in such a relationship. Perhaps you have struggled with addiction. The most important message for either reader is, the alcoholic should not attempt sobriety alone and neither should the family member make the necessary changes in their PATH without proper support. Connect with others in the recovery world for support. Get help! With an enhanced understanding of alcoholism and addiction, and an awareness of your family's reaction and unhealthy enabling, it is time to change. Get help!

The resources I cite in this book were immensely helpful for me. I also found AA to be a solid foundation for alcoholics in recovery, and Al-Anon, the sister organization, to be a helpful foundation for family members of alcoholics. Those fellowships are good places to start with recovery.

There are also a myriad of websites with resources, podcasts, tools, and exercises readily available to the public. These websites may be for treatment centers or recovery communities, which play different roles in the treatment and recovery (post-treatment) process. The following are a few of my favorite websites, grouped into three categories: addiction trends, topics, and challenges; family member services; and safety services (domestic abuse). I anticipate that over time I will post more resources and workshop offerings through my website.

Addiction Trends, Topics, and Challenges:
* hazeldenbettyford.org/professionals/resources/podcasts

Family Member Services:
- hazeldenbettyford.org/treatment/family-children/family-program
- al-anon.org
- coda.org
- melodybeattie.com/coping-tool-kits/
- hazelden.org/store/publicpage/family-support

Safety Services:
- thehotline.org
- justice.gov/ovw/local-resources

I listed the safety services websites because safety from domestic violence is more than physical or sexual abuse. Domestic violence is a pattern of behaviors used to gain or maintain power and control, and I have provided numerous examples throughout this book. To be clear, not all alcoholics partake in physical or sexual abuse, but they do often exercise some behaviors used to gain power or control. To draw from the Duluth model (a program developed to reduce domestic violence against women), an abusive partner uses many tactics to keep a family member in a relationship. I am sharing some of the core points, sometimes altered in my own words, including:

- **Using Emotional Abuse** (putting the family member down, name-calling, playing mind games, and inducing humiliation and guilt).
- **Using Isolation** (controlling what the family member does, who the family member sees and talks to, where the family member goes, and how long he or she can be gone).
- **Minimizing, Denying, and Blaming** (making light of the abuse, shifting responsibility for abusive behavior, and saying the family member caused it or it did not happen at all).
- **Using Children** (inducing guilt related to the children, using the children to relay messages, using visitation to engage in harassment, and threatening to take the children away).
- **Using Gender Privilege** (inducing servitude, controlling decision making, and defining family roles).

- **Using Economic Abuse** (preventing the family member from getting or keeping a job, controlling family assets, and not letting the family member know about or have access to family income or assets).
- **Using Coercion and Threats** (threatening to harm the family member, to leave the relationship, to commit suicide, to make a false report to authorities, and coercing a family member to drop charges or do illegal things).
- **Using Intimidation** (making a family member afraid by using gestures and actions, destroying property, abusing pets, and displaying weapons).

Please don't minimize the behaviors of power and control. These behaviors are abusive. Period! Sometimes my husband would go months without calling me an ugly name or asking me where I was going and when I would be home. And I would let the abuse slide because I didn't believe it was frequent enough to be considered abuse. I excused his behavior at the expense of my dignity, self-esteem, and safety. If you have experienced any of these behaviors of power and control, please get help!

One last point from Stephen Panebianco, MD. Whether you are the person who is struggling with addiction or a family member, friend, or loved one of someone who is struggling with addiction, beyond getting the proper support that is needed, it is also important to cultivate a skillset for emotional regulation. This is possible through mind-body skills acquisition. Our emotional reality is a very powerful force that impacts our overall health, thinking, urges, and behaviors, often on the subconscious level. Therefore, having a skillset to shift your internal state without an unhealthy reliance on something external is a powerful PATHway of awareness to choosing the type of engagement your Rumi visitors have at your guesthouse.

Figure 1

PATH—Life Cycle with an Addict

PARTNERSHIP	ANGER
Sharing Responsibilities	Things "Not Right"
Enjoying Shared Moments	Diminishing Shared Interests
Gathering with Friends and Family	Trying to Change the Addict (Fixing)
Planning Social and Logistical	False Sense of Power and Ego
Open Communication Channels	Spending Less Time with Others
Teamwork Solving Problems	Taking on More Responsibilities
Grateful and Gratitude Expressions	Covering for the Addict (Excuses)
Attentive	Embarrassed by the Addict
Healthy Physical and Sexual Interaction	Unhealthy Exchange through Control and Power
Trusting	Arguing and Yelling
Honest, Kind, and Bonding	Physical Altercations
Mutual Support (Goals and Passions)	Manipulation and Blame
Tapping into the Needs of Others	Push Pull
Shared Respect Including Differences	Running Away and Running Back
Negotiating and Compromise	Hypervigilance
Emotional Sharing ("I feel") and Expression	Bargaining without Addressing Core Issues
Safety and Space	Loss, Isolation, and Aloneness
Thoughtful and Caring Actions	Lack of Presence and Ignoring
Dedicated Shared Time	Peacemaker, Martyr, or Victim
Laughter, Levity, and Intimacy	Secrecy
Forgiveness after Conflict	Lack of Trust (Keeping Tabs)
Apologizing when Appropriate	Lack of Honesty
Healthy Connections with Others	Paranoia, Threats, and Intimidation
Healthy Boundaries	Resentment and Coercion
Respectful Language	Dependency
Honoring Commitments	Judgmental, Critical, and Demeaning

Accepting Responsibility for Actions	Violation and Deep Hurt
Accepting Responsibility for Choices	Passive-Aggressive and Hostility
	Selfishness
	Jealousy and Distrust

TOLERANCE	**HEALING***
Unhappy	Purpose
Unhealthy Patience (with Behavior of the Addict)	Recognition, Restoration, and Rebuilding
Surviving	Autoregulation
Giving in and Giving up	Choice
Acceptance	Truth in Living
Disconnected	Insight
Suppressing Feelings	Clear Communication (Boundaries)
Enduring	Emotional Expression (Sharing)
Loss of Relationship, of Self, and of Will	Reframing (Thoughts) and Refocusing (Perception)
Putting Own Safety at Risk	Self-Care
Emptiness and Hopelessness	Openness
Sadness	Forgiveness
Apathy	Community Connection
Fantasies of Other Life without Intent	Awareness Enhanced
Feeling Trapped	Letting Go
Ignoring	Mind-Body Skills and Meaning
Resignation	AND JOY
Feeling Invisible	
Depending on Others for Social or Emotional Needs	
Worn Down	
Imbalanced	
Paralyzed	

* Acronym for HEALING: PRACTICERS OF CALM AND JOY™

FIGURE 2

The DO NOTs with an Alcoholic

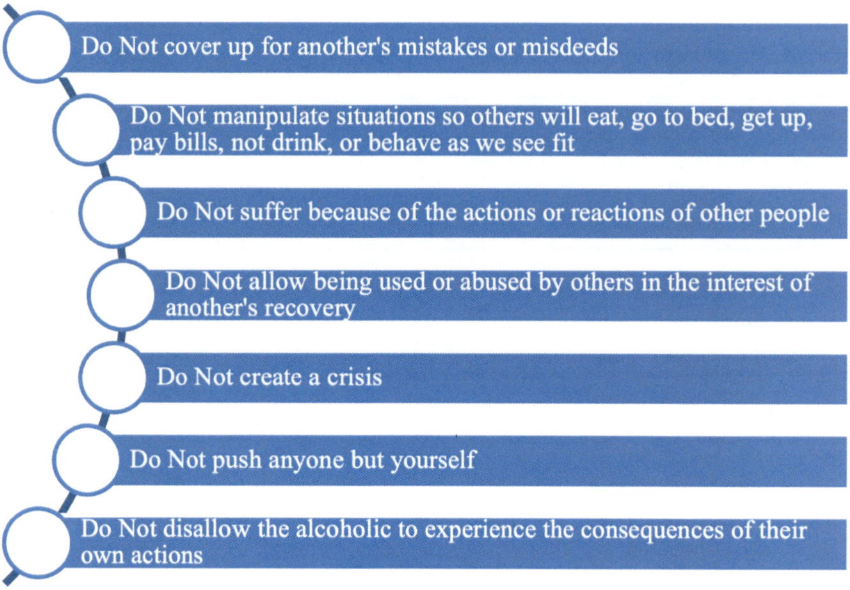

Do Not cover up for another's mistakes or misdeeds

Do Not manipulate situations so others will eat, go to bed, get up, pay bills, not drink, or behave as we see fit

Do Not suffer because of the actions or reactions of other people

Do Not allow being used or abused by others in the interest of another's recovery

Do Not create a crisis

Do Not push anyone but yourself

Do Not disallow the alcoholic to experience the consequences of their own actions

Source: "Detachment," Al-Anon website.

FIGURE 3

The Jellinek Curve

Source: Expert Committee on Mental Health, World Health Organization. Revision including recovery and rehabilitation Dr. Max M. Glatt; revised as the "Glatt Chart" (1958).

BIBLIOGRAPHY

Alexander, Eben. *Proof of Heaven: A Neurosurgeon's Journey into the Afterlife.* New York: Simon & Shuster, 2012.

Beattie, Melody. *Codependent No More: How to Stop Controlling Others and Start Caring for Yourself,* 2nd ed. Center City, Minnesota: Hazelden Publishing, 1992.

"Codependency and Codependent Relationships." BPDFamily.com. Retrieved September 9, 2014. https://bpdfamily.com/content/codependency-codependent-relationships.

Denison, Craig. "The Gifts of the Holy Spirit." First15.org. March 11, 2021. https://www.first15.org/03/11/the-gifts-of-the-holy-spirit/.

"Detachment." Al-Anon Family Groups website. https://al-anon.org/pdf/S19.pdf.

Expert Committee on Mental Health: Alcoholism Subcommittee; Second Report. World Health Organization Technical Report Series No. 48, 1952. https://apps.who.int/iris/bitstream/handle/10665/40186/WHO_TRS_48.pdf?sequence.

Nakken, Craig. *The Addictive Personality: Understanding the Addictive Process and Compulsive Behavior.* Center City, Minnesota: Hazelden Publishing, 1996 [2nd ed.].

P., Wally. *Back to Basics: The Alcoholics Anonymous Beginners' Meetings.* Tucson, Arizona: Faith With Works Publishing Company, 2015 [2nd ed., ninth printing].

Roberts, Elizabeth, and Elias Amidon, eds. *Earth Prayers from Around the World: 365 Prayers, Poems, and Invocations for Honoring the Earth.* New York: HarperCollins, 1991.

Rumi, Jalaluddin. "The Guest House." *Rumi: Selected Poems.* Coleman

Banks, with John Moyne, A. J. Arberry, and Reynold Nicholson, eds. London: Penguin Books, 1995.

Sweisgood, P. "Understanding the Progression of Alcoholism--The Jellinek Chart." *The Journal of the New York State School Nurse Teachers Association*. 1974; 6(1), 17–19. Retrieved September 5, 2020. https://ncbi.nlm.nih.gov/pubmed/4548908.

"The Twelve Steps." Al-Anon Family Groups website. 1996. https://al-anon.org/for-members/the-legacies/the-twelve-steps/.